ADELE
IS LIFE

ADELE IS LIFE

A Superfan's Guide to
All Things We Love about Adele

KATHLEEN PERRICONE
ILLUSTRATED BY LAUREN MORTIMER

CONTENTS

Introduction 7
Part One: Hello, It's Me 11
    When She Was Young 13
    British Invasion 19
    World Wonder 25
    Labor of Love 33
    Life Begins at *30* 39
Part Two: The Golden Years 45
    Discography 47
Part Three: One and Only 69
    Adele to Z 71
Part Four: Someone Like Her 113
    A Relatable Queen 115
    Adele Unfiltered 125
    Anatomy of an Artist 137
    Meme Material 143
    Adele's Playlist 153
Acknowledgments 159
About the Author 159

INTRODUCTION

The Queen of Heartbreak, Adele rules the music charts as the best-selling female artist of the twenty-first century. The pop-soul powerhouse introduced herself in 2008 with "Chasing Pavements" off her debut album, *19*, which earned her three Grammy nominations and the wildest prediction from *Billboard* magazine: "Adele truly has potential to become among the most respected and inspiring international artists of her generation." Just three years later, the English singer took the crown with her next release, *21*—which remains the top album of the twenty-first century with thirty-one million copies sold worldwide. Perhaps even more impressive: only three notches down the list, after *The Eminem Show* and Norah Jones's *Come Away with Me*, is Adele's third album, *25*, with twenty-three million copies sold. Most recently, her fourth album, *30*, was the best-selling album of 2021.

For Adele, it's quality over quantity, as she takes her time between musical projects: Her first four albums, *19*, *21*, *25*, and *30*—each named for her age when she wrote them—were released over a span of thirteen years. "I have to wait for a feeling," the thirty-five-year-old

"It was the most reliable friend I've ever had in my life. There was a song for every emotion, there was a song for every feeling."

explained to *The Hollywood Reporter* in 2023 when asked if fans could expect her fifth album any time soon. "I have nothing to say *yet*."

Two decades ago, she wrote her first song, "Hometown Glory," an ode to the sixteen-year-old's South London suburb, and ever since she has found inspiration in the singular events of her life: heartbreak, new love, motherhood, divorce, and healing. But it's the sincere way she writes about them—and how she emotes the lyrics on tracks like "Someone Like You," "Hello," and "Easy on Me"—that has resonated with millions of fans around the world, from millennials like herself to Gen Zers and baby boomers ("my perfect audience," she joked to *The Hollywood Reporter*). Equally successful commercially and critically, Adele's brand of sentimentality has sold more than 120 million albums and earned her sixteen Grammy Awards, eighteen Billboard Music Awards, five American Music Awards, as well as an Academy Award (Best Original Song for "Skyfall," from the 2012 *James Bond* film of the same name), and a Primetime Emmy for the 2021 CBS special *Adele One Night Only*.

All her life, Adele has had an innate ability to feel deeply, something she refers to as an inherited sadness from her mother, Penny Adkins. Along with this emotional depth, her mother also passed down a love of music. "I was lonely a lot of my childhood, whether it be like, actually or just felt it," Adele revealed to Apple Music's Zane Lowe during her promotion of *30*. "I was just always very available to the way that music made me feel from a very very young age . . . It was the most reliable friend I've ever had in my life. There was a song for every emotion, there was a song for every feeling." Now as an artist, she's making music for anyone who might too need that same reliable friend. "I really think some of the songs on this album could really help people. I think a song like 'Hold On' [about losing hope] could actually save a few lives."

PART ONE

Hello, It's Me

WHEN SHE WAS YOUNG

Many of Adele's earliest memories are tied to music—and her mother, Penny Adkins. There were lullabies at bedtime, and when she was old enough to sing on her own, living room performances with her mother holding up a lamp as her daughter's makeshift spotlight. A week before Adele's fourth birthday in 1992, she attended her first concert, The Beautiful South, when her mother snuck her into London's Brixton Academy by hiding the little girl inside her trench coat. "I couldn't see anything, and there was a bodybuilder who put me on his shoulders," Adele reminisced two decades later on BBC Radio 2. The mystery man didn't just give her the best seat in the house. When the band released balloons from the ceiling, "he walked through the crowd and knocked someone out who wouldn't give me a balloon. It was amazing. It's my clearest memory of when I was little."

Penny Adkins was only eighteen when she gave birth to Adele Laurie Blue Adkins on May 5, 1988, a year after meeting Welsh window cleaner Mark Evans at a pub in North London. Their whirlwind romance fizzled as quickly as it sparked, and the two split before their daughter's first birthday. Evans eventually returned to Wales, two hundred miles (322 km) away, to work as a plumber, and the young single mother gave up her art school aspirations to care for Adele. "She never, ever reminds me of that," the Grammy-winning singer told *The New Zealand Herald* in 2011. "I try to remember it."

Adele and her mother essentially grew up together. Their mother-daughter relationship is more like a best friend relationship. Raising her little girl in South London, Adkins introduced her to many of her favorite musical artists, like The Cure (Adele's second concert, at five), Jeff Buckley, Mary J. Blige, and Lauryn Hill. Adele became obsessed with "Dreams," the 1993 global hit by Gabrielle, a British R&B singer who wore an eyepatch to disguise her drooping eyelid. When her little girl came down with a case of conjunctivitis, Adkins sewed her a custom eyepatch with sequins just like Gabrielle's to wear to school. Even after her pink eye cleared up, Adele continued to sport the medical accessory around the house so she could emulate her favorite singer.

The two didn't have much—Adkins worked odd jobs and they lived in government-subsidized housing—but Adele was rich in unconditional

> *"I was one of those kids that was like, 'I want to be a ballet dancer. No, a saxophone player. No, a weather girl.'"*

love and encouragement. "She's honest and open and so supportive," she gushed about her "hippie mum" to *The Scotsman*. "I was one of those kids that was like, 'I want to be a ballet dancer. No, a saxophone player. No, a weather girl.' And my mum would run me to all these classes. She has always said, 'Do what you want and if you're happy, I'm happy.' She always had to do things whether she wanted to or not to get money to bring me up."

To ease the single mother's burden, Adele's paternal grandfather John Evans also contributed financially to the little girl's care. She spent many school holidays with her beloved "Grampy" exploring seaside towns in Wales, often with her father, Mark Evans, in tow. But at the age of ten, any connection to her father's side of her family ended when her grandfather died of cancer—a loss so devastating Adele needed counseling to work through her grief. "I loved him so much, more than the world," she later confessed to *i-D* magazine. "I was so, so sad." Especially heartbroken for her "Nana," Adele was inspired to become a surgeon and "fix people's hearts." But after studying biology at school, her passion shifted to "fun—and boys," she joked. "I gave up on it." Her father also reeled from the death of his father, spiraling into an alcohol addiction that severed his relationship with his only daughter for two decades. "I'd cut off contact with him when I was ten or eleven," she revealed to *Q* magazine in 2011. "I last saw him at my grandma's funeral. I think I was about fifteen."

By then, Adele was a stand-out talent at the prestigious BRIT School, a vocational institution specializing in performing and creative arts whose graduates—including Amy Winehouse, Leona Lewis, Jessie J, FKA twigs, and Imogen Heap—have collectively sold more than 250 million albums worldwide. At thirteen, she aced her audition by showing off her vocal and musical gifts, singing Stevie Wonder's "Free" and performing an instrumental version of "Tumbledown Blues" by James Rae on the clarinet. In her application, Adele described herself as "someone who's dedicated to music purely through love and passion for it." The BRIT School not only sharpened her natural-born talents, but also taught her practical skills, such as how to use a recording studio and interpret legal contracts. "It's an amazing feeling to wake up and go to school with kids that want to be something," she told *CBS News Sunday Morning* in 2008 when she returned to BRIT for the first time since becoming a platinum-selling artist.

For a class project, Adele recorded a three-track demo of original music: "Hometown Glory," the first song she ever wrote; "Daydreamer"; and "My Same," which a friend uploaded to MySpace, a little-known social-media platform in the UK, in 2005. "But about a year later, all the record companies got on there to look for the next Lily Allen," Adele recalled to *Billboard*. One of those labels was XL, an independent entity with a respectable roster of talent, such as Radiohead singer, Thom Yorke, The White Stripes, and M.I.A. "XL e-mailed me and invited me for a meeting, but I ignored them to focus on finishing school and planning my eighteenth birthday party," she confessed to the magazine with a giggle.

But XL would not give up so easily. Adele's music had eleven thousand plays on MySpace—an impressive number for an unknown teenager still in high school. Anxious that another label might sign her first, XL founder Richard Russell went to see Adele perform at a tiny West London bar, Cherry Jam, so he could properly introduce himself. Onstage with only an acoustic guitar, she "seemed to possess a singularity; vulnerability coupled with complete certainty," Russell wrote in his 2020 memoir, *Liberation Through Hearing*. "She had an intangible but unmistakable aura of originality . . . I was sure of Adele's ability."

In September 2006, XL signed Adele, who Russell described as "punk Barbra Streisand," to her first recording contract, inking the deal at her local pub, The Duke of Wellington. It was the same place where she met, and ultimately dumped, the man who would inspire much of her debut album, *19*. Before the romance, she was plagued by an eight-month period of writer's block. Yet once they split, "the songs just poured out."

BRITISH INVASION

In 2008, the multiplatinum *Back to Black* made Amy Winehouse a household name; Estelle crossed over the Atlantic with her Kanye West collaboration, "American Boy"; and Welsh singer Duffy had everyone begging for "Mercy." That year, the British soul movement also formally introduced its newest talent, Adele, whose debut album, *19*, entered the UK charts at No. 1. In the US, it was a bit of a slow burn as she worked to set herself apart from "the new Amys." "It's big, really big here," Adele admitted to the Associated Press in June 2008. "I feel like I'm riding the [British] wave and I'm proud to be a part of it. I think it's inspiring."

"She just came on the scene personality-wise saying, 'Take me as I am.' There were no apologies with her."

Back in London, it had been a quick ascent for the young singer who began recording her debut album shortly after celebrating her nineteenth birthday in May 2007. A month later, she made her television debut on the BBC's popular music talk show *Later . . . with Jools Holland* to perform "Daydreamer," which introduced the unknown Adele to millions of viewers watching from home. By October, she had completed *19*, set for wide release in January 2008—and music industry experts predicted she would be the year's breakthrough act. She began by cracking the UK, where her first single, "Chasing Pavements," reached No. 2 on the charts and was a Top 10 international hit in nine other countries. In the US, where the song peaked at No. 21, Adele built buzz with a handful of sold-out shows in New York City, Los Angeles, and Austin.

She also made headlines when she abruptly canceled the North American dates of her tour, An Evening with Adele, citing "family issues," when in reality she just wanted to spend more time with her new boyfriend. Later describing the time period as "my E.L.C., my Early Life Crisis," Adele admitted to *Nylon* magazine in 2009 that she regretted the decision, which had been influenced by alcohol. "I'm like, 'I can't believe I did that.' It seems so ungrateful. . . . I was drinking far too much and that was kind of the basis of my relationship with this boy. I couldn't bear to be without him, so I was like, 'Well, OK, I'll just cancel my stuff then.'"

But everything changed on October 18, 2008, when Adele was the musical guest on *Saturday Night Live*. Weeks before the US election, the episode was touted not for host Josh Brolin but for a cameo by someone who had become a lightning rod in America at the time: Republican vice presidential nominee Sarah Palin. An estimated seventeen million people—the show's best ratings in fourteen years—tuned in to watch Palin, yet inadvertently witnessed history as Adele sang "Chasing Pavements" and "Cold Shoulder." The next morning, *19* topped the iTunes charts (an increase in sales by 500 percent) and over the following days climbed thirty-five spots on the *Billboard* 200 chart to No. 11.

"I remember seeing her, and just being blown away, and realizing that I had not paid the attention to her that I should have," remembered *Billboard* West Coast Editor Melinda Newman. "I think I had that realization with several million people at the exact same time. She had a strong command of her singing craft and of her songwriting craft, and she just came on the scene personality-wise saying, 'Take me as I am.' There were no apologies with her." Indeed, backstage that night on *Saturday Night Live*, Adele met Palin, the running mate of Senator John McCain, while wearing a pin showing support for Democratic opponent Barack Obama. She had tried to avoid the politician who insisted she was a "huge fan." "All these Secret Service agents surrounded me," Adele recalled to the *The Boston Globe*, "and I didn't say, 'Go Obama!' like I wanted to."

The twenty-year-old singer ended the year on an even higher note with four Grammy nominations for Record of the Year, Song of the Year, Best Female Pop Vocal Performance—all three for "Chasing Pavements"—as well as Best New Artist. "I had to lock myself in the bathroom for an hour before I could come to terms with it," Adele told *The Minnesota Star Tribune* of the unbelievable news. "It was a world where I never, ever thought I'd be included—not now or in the years to come." Two months later at the awards ceremony, she won a pair of golden gramophones, most notably for Best New Artist, beating out fellow British soulstress Duffy, the Jonas Brothers, Lady Antebellum (now Lady A), and Jazmine Sullivan.

As it turned out, one of the presenters of the award was the British singer, rapper, and actress, Estelle. While many artists endorsed Adele when *19* first came out, Estelle was one of the very few that did not. The singer publicly slugged Adele for not being "soul" enough, however, Adele shrugged off Estelle's criticism in an interview with the Associated Press. Onstage at the Grammys, there was no hint of lingering resentment as Adele hugged Estelle, the first time they had ever met. The Best New Artist win brought the evening full circle: On the red carpet before the show, photographers had asked her to step aside so they could photograph actress Kate Beckinsale. *Vogue* editor Hamish Bowles, who styled Adele in a black satin cocktail dress custom-designed by Barbara Tfank, recalled her expression in that moment. "It was a look that said: By the end of this evening, you will know who I am."

The whole world did by the summer of 2009, as she concluded her first global tour, An Evening with Adele, and effectively ended the era of *19*, an album that had reached the Top 10 in fifteen countries and sold more than 8.5 million copies (3.1 million in the US alone). Along the way, the heartbreak that inspired the album had healed. Two years on, "It seems like a really long time ago," Adele mused to *The Boston Globe*, "and it's strange to be singing songs about someone I don't really care about anymore like that." By then, she had a fresh new ex-boyfriend, reportedly a photographer hired to document her world tour. She had written some new songs, yet didn't feel the pressure to jump back into the studio so quickly just to ride the wave of *19*'s success.

"I'm just trying to make the second record as believable as the first one," she told *Clutch* magazine. "Trying to write about things that are normal rather than things that I'm doing cause what I'm doing now is the least normal thing ever. I'm trying to move on as an artist and develop my sound, get better as a guitar player and a bass player, and get to know my voice better . . . 'Cause the first album was more just like a mashup of all the different music that I like. I hope for more of a defined sound."

WORLD WONDER

Because the success of *19* was so extraordinary, Adele was realistic about how her second album would compare, both commercially and artistically. In interviews, any time she was asked about following up on her debut, she was careful to hedge her bets. "I don't think you come into your own until your second or third record," she told *Billboard* in 2009. "I don't want to get too big too fast and then have to deal with the sophomore curse. It's more important for me to be able to make a lot of good records than to just have one hit and be forgotten."

But unexpectedly, she soon had plenty of inspiration. Near the end of the *19* era, Adele was "blindsided" by her soulmate, a mystery man she has never mentioned by name. Musically, she had the full attention of Rick Rubin: "the most important producer of the last twenty years," according to MTV, he was behind the chart-topping success of everyone from the Beastie Boys and Red Hot Chili Peppers to Jay-Z. The night Adele won Best New Artist at the Grammys, Rubin offered his services—and he had a specific vision. "He came to my Hollywood Bowl show and he said, 'You're so different live. You've got to get your live show across on your record,'" she recalled to Quebec-based QMI Agency. To achieve this, Rubin assembled a band of musicians (guitar, bass, drums, piano) and rejected the use of any electronic instruments.

Before arriving at Rubin's Shangri-La Studio in Malibu, Adele spent months writing and recording demos with a team that included Ryan Tedder and Dan Wilson, who have worked with Beyoncé and Taylor Swift, respectively. On her second album, it was imperative to Adele that she "show growth and development and progression" as an artist—so she studied the generational greats across pop (Dusty Springfield and Alanis Morissette), R&B (Mary J. Blige), hip-hop (Drake), even country (Dolly Parton and Lady Antebellum) and bluegrass (Alison Krauss). "I made a huge effort to just swim in music for a while," she told MSN Music, "just trying to understand what it is about a song that moves me; where it peaks, why I think it peaks, stuff like that, just kind of studying it." Adele applied what she learned, and the result was a collection of songs that accurately conveyed her feelings unlike any before. "Someone Like You," about moving on from a former love, "is one of the most articulate songs I've ever heard in general, let alone one of mine," she bragged to *Rolling Stone*.

> *"I made a huge effort to just swim in music for a while."*

"That's quite a breath of fresh air for me. It's just a bitter break-up record, and towards the end I'm a bit more like, 'Well, shit happens.'"

When it came time to record the final tracks with Rubin, the rollercoaster of emotions took a sharp turn. The producer is known for his unorthodox methods to pull the best performance out of his artists, and Adele was forced out of her comfort zone during the five weeks she was ensconced at Shangri-La, a two-acre compound perched on a cliff overlooking the Pacific Ocean. "I loved being in the studio with Rick. I hated Malibu," she confessed to QMI Agency. "I'm hardly a beach babe. I'm too pale for the sun. I'm allergic to it. I get heat rash. I get blisters all over me. The first day it was overcast. I got sunburnt quite badly, which lasted the entire time. But the studio was amazing. It was like the best thing I've

> *"All of the playing was keying off the emotion on Adele's outrageous vocal performance."*

ever done." In the studio, Rubin had the band play live as Adele recorded her vocals to create an authentic sound. "This was truly an interactive moment where none of the musicians knew exactly what they were going to play and all were listening so, so, deeply and completely to figure out where they fitted in," he explained to *M* magazine. "All of the playing was keying off the emotion on Adele's outrageous vocal performance."

Her intensity was especially palpable during "Rolling in the Deep," which Adele wrote as a "fuck-you" to her ex. "The first time we did [the song], I had to check to make sure it was really her I was hearing coming through my headphones," Smokey Hormel, a session guitarist who's played with Mick Jagger and the Chicks, told *Rolling Stone*. "It sounded like a record as soon as it came out of her mouth. It sounded so perfect. And every time she went back in to do it again, her performance was even better."

When Adele played the completed *21* for label executives, the reaction was so overwhelmingly positive, they pushed back the album's release date several months in order to roll out a massive marketing campaign. In addition to deluxe editions with iTunes and Target, the singer embarked on promotional tours across the US and Europe, hosted online live chats with fans, and appeared everywhere from NBC's *Today* to the *Late Show with David Letterman*. Lead single "Rolling in the Deep" was sent to eight different radio formats, including Adult Top 40, R&B/Hip-Hop, and Alternative—and by the time *21* was released four weeks later in January 2011, the song had been heard by an estimated three *billion* people (nearly half the world population in 2011). The album also enjoyed global domination, topping the charts in thirty countries and selling thirteen million copies in its first year.

But at the height of her record-breaking success, a vocal hemorrhage threatened to take it all away. In November 2011, she canceled the remainder of the Adele Live tour to undergo emergency surgery—and not a moment too soon. "I was singing with damaged vocal chords for three or four months," she revealed to *Billboard*. Although it would take some time to rebuild her soulful voice, there was a silver lining. "It's going to be a lot easier for me to sing now. And mentally, I won't be worried about my voice onstage anymore." Three months later, Adele made her triumphant return at the 2012 Grammy Awards, where she swept the ceremony, winning all six nominated categories: Record of the Year, Album of the Year, Song of the Year ("Rolling in the Deep"), Best Pop Solo Performance ("Someone Like You"), Best Pop Vocal Album, and Best Short Form Music Video ("Rolling in the Deep"). "This record is inspired by something that is really normal and everyone's been through it," a tearful Adele told the audience as she accepted Album of the Year. "It was just a rubbish relationship, and it's gone on to do things that I can't tell you . . . It's been the most life-changing year."

And she wasn't just talking professionally. By Adele's side that night was her new boyfriend, charity entrepreneur Simon Konecki, and the couple had a lot more to celebrate: Adele was secretly two months pregnant. In an interview with *Vogue*, the twenty-three-year-old hinted at her next chapter, revealing she planned to take "four or five years" off to focus on her personal life—which would in turn influence her next album. "If I am constantly working, my relationships fail. So at least now I can have enough time to write a happy record. And be in love and be happy."

ADELE TAKES CENTERSTAGE

In 2011, the singer embarked on her second world tour, Adele Live, and true to its name, all fifty-one performances centered around her sensational voice, with no distractions. The stage design was minimal and modeled after a 1960s jazz club. Adele and her five-piece band were backlit by a wall of ninety-six lampshades (her idea!) with forty-watt household bulbs for moderate illumination, each on its own dimmer switch to set the mood throughout the seventeen-song setlist. For a monochromatic look, "we have gold drapes behind the shades," production designer Rob Sinclair told *Lighting & Sound* magazine. "I wanted to avoid the cliché of red velvet." Fans who didn't snag tickets for the sold-out tour got to experience the magic with the video album *Live at the Royal Albert Hall* released in November 2011, weeks after the superstar was forced to cancel the remaining Adele Live dates due to a vocal hemorrhage. *Live at the Royal Albert Hall* spent sixteen weeks at No. 1 on the DVD charts in the US and went on to sell more than 3 million copies worldwide.

LABOR OF LOVE

Adele took an extended maternity leave following the October 2012 birth of her son, Angelo James Konecki, and there were times she questioned if she should ever return to music for a third album—or let *21* be her epic swan song. "Maybe I should go out on a high. Maybe everyone likes what they've heard of me," she recalled thinking in an AMP Radio interview with Carson Daly in 2015. "And then I realized I want my kid to know what I do. He's really inspired me."

On the eve of Adele's twenty-sixth birthday, in May 2014, she gave fans the gift of a cryptic message on her Instagram that sounded like she was hinting at new music: "Bye bye 25 . . . See you again later in the year." But in October, XL Recording dashed all hope when the label confirmed there were no plans to put out an Adele record that year. In fact, it would be another twelve months before she finally made the announcement everyone was waiting for: *25*, "a make-up record," would be released on November 20, 2015.

Adele actually began working on her third album in early 2013, around the time she won an Academy Award for "Skyfall." But those sessions were soon canceled as she battled writer's block. She tried again months later, flying to New York to work with her "Rumor Has It" songwriting partner, Ryan Tedder. The duo only came up with one song, "Remedy," but she loved it so much and felt creatively reinvigorated. "So I started knocking out some shit songs—they weren't shit—they were good pop songs, but I was just trying to bang it out. I didn't want to think about it," Adele recalled to *i-D*. "And, you know, it got rejected. My manager was like, 'This isn't good enough.' Yeah, it knocked my confidence a bit, but I also knew."

The third time was the charm when Adele returned to the studio at the start of 2014, when her son was a toddler. As she has always written songs about her life, naturally motherhood was her biggest inspiration—but she was self-aware "that's pretty boring for everyone," she admitted to BBC Radio 1's Nick Grimshaw. Her approach was influenced by Madonna's *Ray of Light* (1998), the first album the Material Girl recorded after giving birth to her first daughter Lourdes, "and for me, it's her best," Adele told *Rolling Stone*. "I was so all over the place after having a child, just because

"I was so all over the place after having a child, just because my chemicals were just hitting the fucking roof and shit like that . . ."

my chemicals were just hitting the fucking roof and shit like that . . . I was just drifting away, and I couldn't find that many examples for myself where I was like, 'Fuck, they truly came back to themselves,' until someone was like, 'Well, obviously, *Ray of Light*.'"

One of the first songs Adele wrote was "Hello," a piano ballad not about an ex-boyfriend but herself—and reconnecting with the person that she was before motherhood. "It's a big hello to myself," she explained on AMP Radio. "It's a hello to my fans as well. I think people thought I vanished and it's the other side of *21*. I'm alive, I made it. I didn't crack under the pressure. It's literally a phone call, hello." And as the lead single off *25*, it was the first peek at Adele's long-awaited third album—and she was worried fans would hear it and be more inclined to say "goodbye." Quite the opposite, "Hello" debuted at the top of the *Billboard* Hot 100 in the US, as well as another thirty-five countries, and set a record as the first song to sell over a million digital copies in a week.

When the full album dropped the following month, it was just as historic: *25* sold 3.38 million copies the first week, shattering the record of 2.42 million previously set by *NSYNC's *No Strings Attached* in 2000. Critics were equally impressed. *Entertainment Weekly* described *25* as "a record that feels both new and familiar—a beautiful if safe collection of panoramic ballads and prettily executed detours." *Rolling Stone*, which ranked the album the second-best of the year behind Kendrick Lamar's *To Pimp a Butterfly*, praised Adele's ability to "infuse any line with nuance and power . . . more proof that she's among the greatest interpreters of romantic lyrics."

The least heartbroken of her first three albums, Adele worried that *25* wouldn't resonate with listeners in the same way as *19* and *21* did. "With me being in a brighter space with my love life, will my fans be disappointed in me that I can't fix their broken hearts with a song that is brokenhearted?" she mused to *Rolling Stone*. "I don't want to disappoint them. But at the same time, I can't write a sad record, like, for everyone else. That's not a real record, unless I am sad." However, there are still plenty of tearjerkers on *25*, especially her sentimental second single, "When We Were Young," Adele's favorite song on the album. Set twenty years in the future, the lyrics recall running into an old friend and getting along like no time has passed. Adele wrote it in three days and cried every time she had to rehearse it. "It's just about enjoying each other in that moment and there's a lyric in it that says 'Let me photograph you like this' because it's amazing and this is how I want to remember us," she said on AMP Radio. "The vibe is incredible."

And so were the accolades. In 2016, Adele was named *Billboard*'s Artist of the Year (for the third time), and took top honors at the BRIT Awards, BBC Music Awards, iHeartRadio Music Awards, and Canada's Juno Awards. Just like its predecessor, *25* won all of its nominations at the 2017 Grammys, including the evening's top award, Album of the Year, beating out Beyoncé's *Lemonade*. Five years since she last swept the Grammys, while secretly pregnant, Adele had silenced critics who claimed having a baby at the height of her career would be its death knell. "Always one to go against the grain, it was there and then that I chose to reject the scarcity of success and the idea that you have to be constantly relevant to be successful," she revealed at the 2024 Women in Entertainment Gala, "and that perhaps, just maybe, I could be a hit both on and off the stage. You'll never guess what: I fucking got away with it."

LIFE BEGINS AT 30

In one of her first interviews, nineteen-year-old Adele imagined what she'd be doing at thirty: "Oh I've got everything planned," she told *The Guardian*. "I wanna be settling down by then. And writing pop songs for other people. I've already got ten songs The Pussycat Dolls could sing. But obviously I'm not gonna get in a bikini! So at thirty, I'll have my first bah-bee, be married, have a really nice three-story family house in Clapham with a little picket fence and be writing songs for pop tarts."

In reality, her thirtieth brought the end of her short-lived marriage to Simon Konecki, the father of her then-six-year-old "bah-bee" Angelo. At the time of their separation in early 2019, the family was living five thousand miles from Clapham, London, in a $9.5 million mansion in Beverly Hills next door to actress Jennifer Lawrence. Back in 2017, rumors swirled that Adele had wed Konecki, but the singer later confirmed to *Vogue*, "We got married when I was thirty . . . and then I left." (Less than three weeks after announcing their separation, Adele turned thirty-one.)

That day, she let her Instagram followers know exactly how she was feeling about the milestone—as well as her next chapter. "This is 31 . . . thank fucking god," she captioned a carousel of photos from a birthday celebration with friends. "30 tried me so hard but I'm owning it and trying my hardest to lean in to it all . . . 31 is going to be a big ol' year and I'm going to spend it all on myself. For the first time in a decade, I'm ready to feel the world around me and look up for once."

There were several months between when she actually split from Simon and when she told the world, and Adele used that time to channel her raw emotions into music for her fourth album. She continued to work on it while also working on herself. Over the course of the 2019 year, she embarked on a healing journey that was emotional, mental, and physical: she stopped drinking, went on daily hikes, climbed a mountain in Idaho with friends, and even got into sound bath meditation. During a trip to London, she had songwriting sessions with several hitmakers who worked on *25*, including Max Martin ("Send My Love") and Greg Kurstin ("Hello").

More painful than her divorce was the effect it had on her son. After a conversation with Angelo in which he told her "I can't see you," meaning she wasn't there emotionally, Adele revamped the concept of her "divorce" album. Instead of writing about her own heartbreak, she focused on his—explaining in the lyrics of her songs why she had decided to end her relationship with his father. She asks for forgiveness on "Easy on Me," which became the most streamed song on Spotify the day it was released on October 15, 2021. Adele chose the ballad as *30*'s lead single because she particularly loved its "soaring chorus" and after a six-year hiatus, it "just felt like a me song," she explained on BBC Radio's *Zoe Ball Breakfast Show*. Her comeback was solidified four weeks later when *30* was officially released—and became the best-selling album of 2021 its very first day.

By this time, Adele had a new muse: Rich Paul, a sports agent who represents A-list athletes including NBA superstar LeBron James. The two had met years earlier at a party when Adele was "a bit drunk" and made a joke about him signing her to his roster, and reconnected in 2021 as Adele was finalizing her divorce from Simon. "Oh, he's so funny, he's hilarious," she gushed to Oprah about her new boyfriend. "And very smart. You know, he's very, very smart. It's quite incredible watching him do what he does."

A year into the relationship, Adele sparked engagement rumors when she wore a massive diamond ring at the 2022 BRIT Awards. "As if I would ever tell anyone if I was or wasn't," she teased days later on *The Graham Norton Show* as the camera zoomed in on the pear-shaped rock. "It's lovely though, isn't it?" The following year, at her Weekends with Adele residency in Las Vegas, the singer ignited a whole new round of media frenzy when she referred to Rich as "my husband." She finally set the record straight in August 2024 when a fan at an Adele in Munich concert asked her to marry him. "I can't marry you," she replied, holding up her left hand to show the diamond ring on her finger, "cause I'm already getting married!"

Domestic bliss seemed on the horizon for Adele after concluding nearly two years of Vegas performances. When she looked ahead to 2025 and beyond, she did not see new music in her future. Instead, the thirty-six-year-old singer hoped to expand her family with Rich Paul, who has three children of his own from previous relationships. "Once I'm done with all of my obligations and all of my shows, I want to have a baby," she told fans at a Weekends with Adele concert in May 2024. "And I want to have a girl because I've already got a boy . . . With me as her mother and Rich as her father, my daughter's going to be a bossy little queen, isn't she?"

Time out of the spotlight to recharge and find inspiration for her next album has always served Adele, who took six years off after *25* to focus on being a mother and wife before returning with her next album. This time around, she hopes to flex other artistic muscles. "I want a big break after all this and I think I want to do other creative things just for a little while," she admitted to German network ZDF ahead of her monthlong Adele in Munich residency in August 2024. Although she didn't specify her plans, in late 2023 the singer did discreetly trademark a business brand, The Shelbourne Collective, in the UK. Filed under the 74100 label, she would be permitted to produce "specialized design activities," which could include cosmetics, fashion, accessories, even home decor, according to *Forbes*.

But not to worry—Adele's first love (after her son, of course) will always be music. "I would never be able to give up singing and writing songs," she told ZDF, even if she could do without the downside of it. "I don't like being famous, [but] I love that I get to make music all the time, whenever I want, and people are receptive to it and like it . . . The fact that people are so interested in my voice and my songs is pretty wild."

CLOSER TO 40

While still promoting her first album back in 2009, Adele was already being bombarded with questions about when she'd put out her second. "I'm not in a rush," she replied to *The Boston Globe*. "I think it's great that people liked my first album, but I hope they'll be around in twenty years and like my fourth and fifth albums, too." By those calculations, fans could expect the follow-up to 30 sometime around 2028—when she'll be forty. "I just don't think I'm gonna write an album for quite some time," Adele admitted to fans at her Las Vegas residency in January 2024. Two hours of singing each night is hard enough on her voice, she didn't want to wear it out by also spending her days in the recording studio, she added in an interview with *The Hollywood Reporter*. "I have to wait for a feeling. If I get antsy, that's when I know I have to go to the studio, and I am the opposite of antsy right now."

PART TWO

The Golden Years

DISCOGRAPHY

The highs and lows of Adele's watershed ages—19, 21, 25, and 30—have been immortalized in her four albums, as she's evolved from heartbroken teen to wife and mother, and ultimately, divorcée. Her sentimental body of work has sold more than 120 million copies worldwide and earned the English superstar quite a trophy collection: eighteen Billboard Music Awards, sixteen Grammy Awards, twelve BRIT Awards, five American Music Awards, and on and on. "Sometimes I don't know what possesses me to do it because albums are like photographs, they're forever," Adele admitted to QMI Agency.

19

ADELE'S "HEARTBROKE SOUL" STIRS UP EMOTIONS
RELEASE DATE: JANUARY 28, 2008

• TRACK LIST •

1. Daydreamer
2. Best for Last
3. Chasing Pavements
4. Cold Shoulder
5. Crazy for You
6. Melt My Heart to Stone
7. First Love
8. Right as Rain
9. Make You Feel My Love
10. My Same
11. Tired
12. Hometown Glory

FIRST LOVES: Adele earned her title as "Queen of Heartbreak" beginning with her very first album, *19*, a collection of melancholic songs detailing the demise of a six-month relationship, when she was nineteen years old. But there's one track that originated the night of her eighteenth birthday, after Adele professed her love to a bisexual male friend. He admitted he felt the same—but then left the party with another man. "I was [like], 'We're not even going out yet and you've cheated on me already!' So 'Daydreamer' is about everything I wanted him to be. The daydream of him," she explained to *The Guardian*. The lead track on *19* also inspired the name adopted by Adele's fandom: Daydreamers.

PUNCH-DRUNK LOVE: Adele's breakthrough single, "Chasing Pavements," is about questioning her dead-end relationship. She wrote it late one night after being tossed from a bar for slapping the aforementioned boyfriend when she learned he had been cheating on her. Assuming she would get into trouble, she took off running down the street, yet when she looked back, "no one was chasing after me," she explained to *Elle* in 2023. "And I was like, 'You're chasing pavements, it's going nowhere.'" That night, Adele recorded the lyrics on her phone and finished composing it in just one day with producer Francis "Eg" White.

"Chasing Pavements" took her in the opposite direction: the second single of *19* reached the Top 10 in eight countries and won a Grammy for Best Female Pop Vocal Performance, one of its three nominations in 2009.

EMOTIONAL ROLLERCOASTER: Adele went through all the feels during her breakup—and she detailed each one on *19*. "Cold Shoulder" imagines what it's like to be the other woman her boyfriend cheated with, set to an upbeat sound produced by Mark Ronson, who had also worked with Amy Winehouse and Lily Allen. Their first meeting was "the most awkward," Adele recalled to *Blues & Soul*, because he was late, and she had passed the time drinking and watching episodes of *The Jerry Springer Show*. But none of that mattered when she pressed play on her demo of "Cold Shoulder," a piano ballad at the time. "I was so blown away and impressed by how already what a strong vision she had of what she wanted for her record," Ronson told *Rolling Stone*. "To be honest, the demo is pretty amazing—just her on the Wurlitzer."

Adele's favorite song on *19* is "Melt My Heart to Stone," which she tearfully wrote in one take about "giving everything for someone, which is what love is all about," she mused to *The Guardian* for its list "1000 Songs Everyone Must Hear." Adele also spoke about her song, "Crazy for You," which she deemed the "only really nice song" on the album. "There's nothing bad in that song, it's just about adoring someone. I wrote it when I was meant to be putting together songs for my album, but I couldn't because I was acting like an idiot, falling to pieces. You're like a fool when you're in love, you do things you shouldn't."

COVER ARTIST: The only song on the album Adele didn't write is "Make You Feel My Love," a cover of Bob Dylan's 1997 standard, which she hadn't heard until her manager, "the biggest Dylan fan," suggested she record it for *19*. "I was being quite defiant against it," Adele recalled to *Premiere*. "I said, 'I don't want a cover on my album. It kind of implies that I'm incapable of writing enough of my own songs for my first record.' And then I heard it in New York when he played it for me, and it just really touched me. It's cheesy, but I think it's just a stunning song, and it really just summed up everything that I'd been trying to write in my songs." In addition to Adele, other artists who have covered "Make You Feel My Love" include Billy Joel, Garth Brooks, Kelly Clarkson, Pink, Neil Diamond, Boy George, and Michael Bolton.

A WAY WITH WORDS: Adele's powerful pipes are of course what first got her noticed, but her often-overlooked songwriting is what has always truly made her proud. With *19*, she had liquid courage to dive deep into her heartbreak, as she grieved the loss of her first great love. "If I'd been in the same frame of mind as I am when I'm talking to you now—i.e. sober!—I probably wouldn't have written any of it," she admitted to *Blues & Soul* magazine. "But yeah, as cheesy as it sounds, I did write to kinda cleanse myself and get it all out of my system really. You know, I hate—I'm actually offended by—literal easy lyrics that have no thought behind them and are purely written because they rhyme. So I do always want my lyrics to be mature and thoughtful. And, while I've personally now stopped listening to my album because I sing it every day, ultimately I do think it is sincere . . . I was very sad when I wrote it. And I think that genuinely does come through in the music."

POPULAR DEMAND: In support of *19*, the singer embarked on her very first tour, An Evening with Adele, seventy-eight shows throughout the UK and North America. At the start in January 2008, the venues were fairly intimate, such as Hotel Café in Los Angeles, which has a capacity of two hundred people. Fifteen months later, the tour ended at the historic Hollywood Bowl with nearly eighteen thousand fans in attendance—and Chaka Khan as her opening act. "I feel like Beyoncé or something," Adele gushed to the cheering crowd. "There's so many of you!"

CHASING CHARTS: The album *19* did numbers: Adele's debut sold over 8.5 million copies worldwide, reaching No. 1 on the UK charts and the Top 10 in fifteen other countries including the US.

21

HELL HATH NO FURY LIKE A WOMAN SCORNED
RELEASE DATE: JANUARY 24, 2011

• TRACK LIST •

1. Rolling in the Deep
2. Rumour Has It
3. Turning Tables
4. Don't You Remember
5. Set Fire to the Rain
6. He Won't Go
7. Take It All
8. I'll Be Waiting
9. One and Only
10. Lovesong
11. Someone Like You
12. I Found a Boy (iTunes Store bonus track)

HEALING JOURNEY: Coming off the heartbreak of *19*, Adele was in love (with a mystery man ten years her senior) and intended to use the romance as inspiration for a more upbeat follow-up to her debut album. In April 2009, she headed into the studio, but after two weeks she had only come up with one song—and it was yet another downer, "Take It All," about not being loved by someone. The writing was on the wall: Two weeks later, Adele's boyfriend ended the eighteen-month relationship, leaving her feeling all the emotions. "I was really angry, then I was bitter, then I was really lonely, and then I was devastated," she confessed to *People*. "It was in that order."

SOMEONE LIKE HIM: The breakup was so devastating to Adele, nearly two years later when she released *21*, she *still* wasn't over her ex. "It's going to take me ten years to recover, I think, from the way I feel about my last relationship," she told MTV News. "It was the biggest deal in my entire life to date . . . He made me totally hungry . . . He was older, he was successful in his own right, whereas my boyfriends before were my age and not really doing much. He got me interested in film and literature and food and wine and traveling and politics and history, and those were things I was never, ever interested in. I was interested in going clubbing and getting drunk."

Adele had finished recording *21* when she learned of her ex's engagement, and was inspired to write "Someone Like You," about moving on after hearing he had done the same. "It's heartbreaking, that song. Even though I wrote it, I can't help but cry every time I hear it," she told *BlackBook* in 2011. "It's my favorite song that I've ever written, because it's so articulate. It completely sums up how I felt then. It's a hopeful song as well as a sad song."

UNCONDITIONAL LOVE: Adele spent five weeks ensconced at Rubin's Malibu studio at the Shangri-La to record this album, an isolating experience that made the British singer miss her mother Penny back in England. To ease her homesickness, she recorded a cover of "Lovesong" by The Cure, one of her mother's favorite bands. But when Adele revealed her version of the goth-rock ballad, it had more of a Bossa nova feel, "she was mortified," the singer told *Variety*. "Then I played it for her, and she loved it and she cried, but the [initial] thought of someone ruining a Cure song fills her with despair. She'd disown me if she didn't like it, but she loved it."

TEAM HEARTBREAK: It was all hands on deck to translate Adele's raw emotions into a musical masterpiece. She enlisted some of the best songwriters in the business, including OneRepublic's Ryan Tedder ("Rumour Has It") and Semisonic frontman Dan Wilson ("Someone Like You"). Within twenty-four hours of her breakup, Adele was on the phone with Paul Epworth, best known at the time for working with Florence + the Machine. She wanted to get into the studio immediately to finish a ballad the two had started the previous year. However, when Epworth met with Adele, "I was ready to murder," she joked to the QMI Agency, and he insisted she channel that energy into "a fierce tune." The newly-single singer was so angry, she could feel her heart racing—which Epworth mimicked with a drum beat on what would become *21*'s lead single, "Rolling in the Deep."

Once demos of all the tracks were completed, production was handed over to the legendary Rubin, who, as mentioned earlier, has worked with everyone from Jay-Z to Metallica. But ultimately, Adele was unhappy with the polished product, feeling it lacked the emotion captured in the original recordings, and she made the decision to scrap all but four of Rubin's tracks. *21* went on to win Album of the Year at the 2012 Grammys, an award shared by Adele and her songwriting team including Rubin.

LITTLE BIT COUNTRY: Adele's time spent touring America for *19* had a lasting impression. During that time, she grew close with the driver of her tour bus, a Nashville native who introduced her to country and bluegrass artists like Garth Brooks, Dolly Parton, Wanda Jackson, and Rascal Flatts. She was immediately drawn to the songwriting: "It's just stories, which to me is what music is about," she explained to CMT. "It's something that has totally rubbed off on the way I write now and this new record." The influence can be heard most clearly on the country-tinged "Don't You Remember," inspired by Lady A's "Need You Now," which was a radio hit while Adele was making *21*. She loved the song so much, she performed it with Darius Rucker at the 2010 CMT Artist of the Year Awards weeks before her album's release.

BURNING UP THE CHARTS: Her song "Set Fire to the Rain" was the third consecutive No. 1 single off *21*, a power-pop ballad that exceptionally complemented Adele's vocals. Outside of the US and UK, the song reached the Top 10 in another two dozen countries. And the flame just wouldn't go out: Two years after its release, Adele's live performance of "Set Fire to the Rain" at the Royal Albert Hall earned her a second Grammy for Best Pop Solo Performance.

SEVENTH HEAVEN: The album, *21* sold an astounding thirty-one million copies worldwide, making it the best-selling album of the twenty-first century—and the seventh-best of all time, behind Led Zeppelin's *Led Zeppelin IV*, Michael Jackson's *Bad and Dangerous*, Alanis Morissette's *Jagged Little Pill*, the *Dirty Dancing* soundtrack, and Celine Dion's *Falling Into You*. In the US, *21* held the No. 1 spot on the *Billboard* 200 chart for twenty-four weeks, the longest ever for a female solo artist.

COMING OF AGE

For Adele, *19* added up to success, so she kept on counting, naming her subsequent albums *21*, *25*, and *30*, her age during the production of each one. That wasn't always the plan though. For her second album, the singer considered *Rolling in the Deep* after its lead single, but ultimately settled on *21* to describe her growth spurt as both an artist and a person. "I deal with things differently now," she said in a press release. "Something that comes with age I think." By *25*, she had grown into a wife and mother, a life-defining event worthy of being catalogued in her discography. But it would be the last album to be titled after her age, she insisted. Six years and a divorce later, however, Adele named her fourth album *30*. "I can change my mind," she joked to NPR in 2021. "You know, I think the age thing is a bloody good idea. And so, I want to keep going with [the titles]. Or I might not."

25

HER ONE AND ONLY MAKE-UP ALBUM
RELEASE DATE: NOVEMBER 20, 2015

• TRACK LIST •

1. Hello
2. Send My Love (To Your New Lover)
3. I Miss You
4. When We Were Young
5. Remedy
6. Water Under the Bridge
7. River Lea
8. Love in the Dark
9. Million Years Ago
10. All I Ask
11. Sweetest Devotion

US TARGET AND JAPAN EDITION BONUS TRACKS

12. Can't Let Go
13. Lay Me Down
14. Why Do You Love Me

FUTURE NOSTALGIA: After two back-to-back breakup albums, Adele healed her own heart with a "make-up album." At the time, she was a new mother and in a committed relationship with her son's father, Simon Konecki, so her songwriting focused more on reconciling the past for a better future. "Making up for lost time. Making up for everything I ever did and never did," she explained in an open letter to fans on Twitter (now X). "But I haven't got time to hold on to the crumbs of my past like I used to.

What's done is done. Turning twenty-five was a turning point for me, slap bang in the middle of my twenties. Teetering on the edge of being an old adolescent and a fully-fledged adult . . . *25* is about getting to know who I've become without realizing. And I'm sorry it took so long, but you know, life happened."

KEEP IN TOUCH: At first listen, the album's lead single, "Hello," sounds like another Adele ballad about heartbreak, regret, and trying to move on in life. This time, however, the twenty-five-year-old was not yearning for a former boyfriend, especially not the ex who inspired *21*. "If I were still writing about him, that'd be *terrible*," she told *Rolling Stone*. "'Hello' is as much about regrouping with myself, reconnecting with myself." As for the line in the chorus "hello from the other side," she explained it's not something morbid "like I'm dead. But it's actually just from the other side of becoming an adult, making it out alive from your late teens, early twenties."

Adele's message was well received by fans: "Hello" topped the charts in thirty-six countries. In the US, it became the fastest-selling digital single with one million copies its first week—during which it was streamed 61.6 million times. "Hello" also single-handedly added three more Grammy Awards to Adele's collection in 2017, with Record of the Year, Song of the Year, and Best Pop Solo Performance.

READY TO POP: During a creative lull, Adele was having lunch in New York with songwriting partner Ryan Tedder when a song playing overhead in the restaurant caught her ear: "I Knew You Were Trouble" by Taylor Swift. "I was like, 'Who did this?' I knew it was Taylor, and I've always loved her, but this is a totally other side, like, 'I want to know who brought that out in her,'" Adele recalled to NPR. Tedder replied it was Max Martin, only the biggest hitmaker in pop music—but Adele had never heard of the Swedish producer, best known for Britney Spears's ". . . Baby One More Time" and "It's Gonna Be Me" by *NSYNC. "I Googled him, and I was like, 'He's literally written every massive soundtrack of my life.'"

Martin of course knew who Adele was and flew to London to meet with her about an unfinished song that had been kicking around in her head since the age of thirteen, "Send My Love (To Your New Lover)," a kiss-off to a bad boyfriend. Martin helped Adele finish it once and for all, putting a pop-R&B spin on the track and turning it into an up-tempo standout on *25*. In a full-circle moment, Tedder's band OneRepublic covered "Send My Love (To Your New Lover)" during a 2016 appearance on BBC Radio 1.

AGAINST ALL ODDS: As she struggled with writer's block, Adele reached out to one of the greatest hitmakers of the 1980s: Phil Collins. In 2013, the two English singers met to discuss a song that Adele wanted him to finish, "and then I just chickened out of everything," she confessed to *Rolling Stone*. The Genesis lead singer, who achieved even greater success as a solo artist with hits like "In the Air Tonight," was initially left in the dark when Adele ghosted him, unaware that she was a new mother. "I sent her an email asking, 'Am I waiting for you, or are you waiting for me?'" he recalled to *Billboard*. Adele eventually replied, telling Collins there was a lot going on in her life at the moment. When *25* came out, she did an interview and admitted, "I was too scared" to work with Collins—which was music to his ears. "That's better than 'He was terrible,'" Collins reasoned to *Billboard*. "I was very grateful for her gentle way of looking at it."

NEW SOUND: Despite her matured outlook on life, Adele made a concerted effort to modernize her sound on *25* for a younger audience, with synthesizers, keyboards, electric drum pads, even a tambourine (played by Haim bassist Este Haim). The biggest departure is on "River Lea," an electric guitar–infused gospel song produced by Danger Mouse, best known for working with Gorillaz, Beck, and The Black Keys. "This time, it was about trying to come up with the weirdest sounds that I could get away with," Adele's longtime producer Paul Epworth told *Rolling Stone*. "This album feels like it fits in maybe more with the cultural dialogue instead of being anachronistic to it. It's almost like she's trying to beat everyone else at their own game."

RECORD BREAKERS: Despite the historic numbers of *21*, Adele didn't feel much pressure to replicate its success with *25*. If anything, it made it easier because there was zero expectation for her to make lightning strike twice. "It's phenomenal what happened with that, but it is a phenomenon," she explained to Nick Grimshaw. "I can't really include it in any expectations of anything I ever do again." Still, she came pretty close: *25* went on to sell over 23.3 million copies, making it the second-best-selling album of the 2010s—behind her own *21*.

GLOBAL DOMINATION: It's not just Adele's albums that break records. Her world tour, Adele Live 2016, sold out everywhere within minutes as online queues overflowed with millions more people than available tickets. In Los Angeles, her eight-night run at Staples Center broke Taylor Swift's previous record of five consecutive sold-out shows—and as of 2024, she still holds the title. Adele Live 2016 entertained 2.5 million people over its sixteen-month trek across three continents, earning $278.4 million.

30

OVERCOMING A "YEAR OF ANXIETY"
RELEASE DATE: NOVEMBER 19, 2021

• TRACK LIST •

1. Strangers by Nature
2. Easy on Me
3. My Little Love
4. Cry Your Heart Out
5. Oh My God
6. Can I Get It
7. I Drink Wine
8. All Night Parking
   (with Erroll Garner)
9. Woman Like Me
10. Hold On
11. To Be Loved
12. Love Is a Game

TARGET EDITION BONUS TRACKS

13. Wild Wild West
14. Can't Be Together
15. Easy on Me
    (with Chris Stapleton)

EMOTIONAL ROLLERCOASTER: An album about the aftermath of her divorce from Simon Konecki, *30* takes the listener along on Adele's emotional journey through heartbreak, regret, shame, anxiety, and ultimately, hope. The twelve-song track list plays out in chronological order, beginning with her decision to leave her husband on "Strangers by Nature" and concluding with finding love again on "Love Is a Game." Nearly halfway through the album, her anxiety begins to subside by Track 5,

"Oh My God." Adele wrote it after the first time she left the house for a night out with her girlfriends—and someone flirted with her. "I was like, 'do you mind? I'm married.' And my friends were like, 'but you're not,'" she recalled on the *Audacy Check-In* podcast. "And I was like, 'oh shit. Okay, oh my God.'"

During an Instagram Live chat with fans, Adele explained *30*'s arc: "I feel like this album is self-destruction, then self-reflection, and then sort of self-redemption." It's so personal, she even considered not putting it out into the world. "'Maybe I don't need to put this album out. Like maybe I should write another,'" she recalled thinking in an Apple Music interview. "When something is more powerful and overwhelming than me, I like to go to a studio because it's normally a basement and there's no fucking windows and no reception, so no one can get ahold of me . . . And no one would've known I'd written that record. And it's like maybe I just had to get it out of my system and stuff."

HARD TIMES: More than just a divorce album, *30* is Adele's way of explaining to her son, Angelo, who was seven-years-old when she split from Konecki in 2019, why she decided to leave his father. She imagined him listening in his twenties or thirties and understanding "who I am and why I voluntarily chose to dismantle his entire life in the pursuit of my own happiness," she revealed to *Vogue*. "It made him really unhappy sometimes. And that's a real wound for me that I don't know if I'll ever be able to heal." Adele tried her best with "Easy on Me," the album's lead single, in which she begs Angelo to forgive her. The concept came to the singer in the shower after a conversation with friends who advised her to "go easy on yourself, don't beat yourself up too much about your decisions," she told *Elle*. "It just really, really stuck with me that, like, I have to be kind to myself."

To help her son through his own feelings, Adele had regular conversations with Angelo before bedtime. Sometimes, she couldn't remember what she had said—and if it was the "right" thing—which spiked her anxiety, so her therapist suggested recording the talks. When she listened back, she was relieved. But more so, what the boy said had a profound effect on his mother and fueled her creativity in the studio. Adele chose to weave snippets of their conversations into "My Little Love," the R&B lullaby she wrote for her son. "He needs to know everyone goes through it," she told *Rolling Stone*. "He's a Libra, so he is, like, 'Chill. It's fine, Mama. Just chill out.'"

LIKE A FINE WINE: Adele let her ego go on "I Drink Wine," a gospel-ish song that was inspired by '70s Elton John—and originally fifteen minutes long! "I took everything so personally at that period of time in my life, so the lyric 'I hope I learn to get over myself' is like [me saying] 'Once I've done that, then maybe I can let you love me,'" she explained to *Rolling Stone*. In the studio, she pulled a "Barry Manilow trick," singing each chorus differently and impersonating various characters when recording the background vocals. "It made it less intimidating because some of the things I'm talking about really hit home for a lot of people." The video for "I Drink Wine" was equally campy: Adele, clad in a glitzy Valentino gown, floats down a river with a glass of wine in her hand as she encounters a happy couple, synchronized swimmers, and hunky fishermen. "It's probably my favorite music video I've ever done," she told fans at its premiere livestream event, Happy Hour with Adele.

BOND GIRL

It's an honor only a handful of performing artists share: singing the *James Bond* theme song. Adele joined the ranks of Paul McCartney, Tina Turner, and Madonna when she wrote and recorded "Skyfall" for the 2012 film of the same name. To filmmakers, the pop-soul singer was the perfect choice to capture the moody drama of the spy franchise, especially for its fiftieth anniversary. "Stylistically, it just felt right to bring back that classic Shirley Bassey feel that you associate with those early Bond films," Sony president of worldwide music, Lia Vollack, told *Variety*. Adele and producer Paul Epworth only had *Skyfall*'s script to use as inspiration for their orchestral pop-soul ballad, with lyrics romanticizing Bond's relationship with his country and MI6 secret intelligence agency. The day they recorded a seventy-seven piece string section "was one of the proudest moments of my life," Adele said in a statement about "Skyfall," which won an Oscar, Grammy, and Golden Globe. "I'll be back-combing my hair when I'm sixty, telling people I was a Bond girl back in the day, I'm sure!"

SOUNDTRACK TO LIFE: Amid her own life's drama, Adele found inspiration in the true story of Judy Garland, the Hollywood entertainer whose personal life was mired by divorce and alcoholism. After watching the biopic *Judy* starring Renée Zellweger, Adele wrote "Strangers by Nature," a cinematic song with organs and strings, with Oscar-winning Swedish composer Ludwig Göransson. Another Old Hollywood classic, *Breakfast at Tiffany's*, influenced the singer to add some retro flair to the seven-minute opus "Love Is a Game." Audrey Hepburn's 1961 romantic-drama was playing on mute in the studio when Adele had hit a creative block. "We were trying to work out how to end the song, and I said, 'We should write it as if we were writing the soundtrack—you know, at the end of the movie, where it pans out,'" she recalled to *Vogue*.

BEST FRIENDS FOREVER: Throughout her "year of anxiety," Adele's friends were her greatest support system. At her lowest points, the one thing they always told her was "just hold on." The piece of advice stuck with her as she was writing *30* and inspired one of its heaviest tracks, "Hold On," about losing hope. So, when it came time to record it, she asked them to be the background vocalists for the chorus, instead of a professional choir. Listening back to it after they left, "I thought they were going to sound terrible," Adele admitted to Apple Music's Zane Lowe, "but they actually sound amazing on it." She's yet to identify the talented bunch, only listing them in the album's liner notes as "Adele's crazy friends."

PRESSING PAUSE: Released six years after *25*, *30* was initially slated for 2020. In February of that year, Adele let it slip at a friend's wedding that her new album would drop "in September," but just weeks later the world went into lockdown due to COVID-19. The necessary finishing touches, like orchestral elements, now couldn't happen due to social distancing and safety mandates. "I'm quarantining. Wear a mask and be patient," she told a fan on Instagram that June. It would be another seventeen months before *30* was finally released, and during that time Adele got to know the material on a deeper level before sharing it with the world. "It was definitely actually in the end quite a nice thing," she admitted on the *Audacy Check-In* podcast. "Everything happens for a reason."

MOST ANTICIPATED: Fans waited six long years for new Adele music, and they proved how badly she was missed: Within a week of her announcing *30*, it became the most pre-added album ever on Apple Music. Its debut was just as monumental, at No. 1 in twenty-five countries with more sales than the rest of the Top 40 albums combined—the best opening week for a female artist since *25*. Around the world, *30* was the best-selling album of 2021, with 5.54 million copies sold.

PART THREE

One and Only

ADELE TO Z

Adele is an open book: she bears her soul on her albums and is unfiltered in interviews. Still, there are many things that fans (nicknamed Daydreamers) don't know about the superstar: the story behind her alter-ego, bond with her pets, beauty secrets, net worth and real estate portfolio, intricacies of her insane vocal range, and what the singer's zodiac sign reveals about her personality. So, inspired by Adele's favorite pop group, the Spice Girls, here's the story from A to Z...

"Then she popped in looking gorgeous, and said, 'You're amazing! When I listen to you I feel like I'm listening to God.' Can you believe she said that?"

ALTER EGO

Beyoncé isn't the only superstar with an alter ego. Like the "Texas Hold 'Em" singer, Adele invented a stage persona to help dispel her stage fright: Sasha Carter, named after Bey's Sasha Fierce and country icon June Carter Cash. The idea actually came about after Adele met Queen Bey, one of her idols, during the *21* era. As she anticipated the life-changing moment, "I had a full-blown anxiety attack," Adele recalled to *Rolling Stone* in 2011. "Then she popped in looking gorgeous, and said, 'You're amazing! When I listen to you I feel like I'm listening to God.' Can you believe she said that? Afterwards, I went out on the balcony crying hysterically, and I said, 'What would Sasha Fierce do?' That's when Sasha Carter was born."

Adele never got to meet the inspiration for her alter ego's Carter surname, who passed away in 2003, just months before her husband of thirty-five years, singer Johnny Cash. However, she does occasionally dress as the five-time Grammy winner: Adele has several '50s-style casual gowns in her wardrobe that she refers to as her "June Carter clothes"—one of which she wore when she dressed up as the country star for Halloween in 2019. Adele, who regularly wears wigs onstage, also named one of her hair pieces "June" after her style idol.

BURBERRY

The first major fashion house to dress Adele was Burberry, whose chief creative officer at the time, Christopher Bailey, designed a midnight blue velvet gown for the full-figured singer to wear at the 2012 Grammys, the night she swept the awards show with six wins. The following year, when the four-months-postpartum singer was up for an Oscar, Adele again tapped Bailey, who she said on her Instagram, "always collaborated with my insecurities to create outfits for me that . . . made me feel fucking great."

So, when it came time to embark on the Adele Live world tour in 2016, the superstar commissioned Bailey to exclusively design her show's statement piece, a long-sleeved sparkling black gown that she wore for each of the hundred-plus concerts. According to Adele's stylist, Gaelle Paul, she wanted "one great dress that went the extra mile and that really wowed"—and that's precisely what Bailey created. The garment's fabric was a flower print done in sequins flowing in different directions to create a galaxy-star effect that Paul told *Billboard* "sparkled like mad" under stage lights.

There were no sequins under Adele's arms; however, the sound of the tiny discs rubbing together could be picked up by her microphone. The dress was also hemmed to an exact length so it barely skimmed the floor and would not soak up any of the water that poured down around the singer during "Set Fire to the Rain." But just in case there were any wardrobe malfunctions out on the road, Bailey and his team hand-made ten copies of the Adele Live gown.

CACKLE

Adele's laugh is as powerful—and iconic—as her pipes! In one of her earliest interviews, with *The Guardian*, the reporter described a moment in which the nineteen-year-old mocked herself for giving the peace sign, as she "cackles like a cockney barmaid." The sound is so LOL-worthy, on TikTok alone there are dozens of video compilations of the singer laughing on TV, during concerts, in the middle of speeches, even while chatting with her fiancé, Rich Paul, courtside at a basketball game. There are nuances to the "Adele cackle," as presented in a four-minute YouTube video titled "The Many Laughing Styles of Adele," including breathless giggle fits and full-bodied guffaws as she throws her head back.

Sometimes, it's hard to contain the cackle. While hosting *Saturday Night Live* in 2020, Adele broke character several times, laughing at herself (the line "lush dangly foliage" gave her pause during the "Africa Tourism" skit) and especially at comedian Kate McKinnon, who played Madame Vivelda, a psychic set in pre-pandemic 2019 who saw only "adult coloring books" in her future for the next year.

Adele was ready to smile again after coming out on the other side of her painful divorce. "I didn't belly laugh for about a year—and my laugh

> *"I didn't belly laugh for about a year—and my laugh is such a big part of who I am."*

is such a big part of who I am," she confessed to Apple Music's Zane Lowe in 2021. Looking back, Adele could actually laugh at all the nonpersonal things that make her cry, both sad and happy tears: random acts of kindness, HBO's *Euphoria*, and her own CBS special, *One Night of Adele* ("I was like, 'oh, thank fucking God' [it turned out so well]"). "My favorite is when you laugh so hard, it turns into tears."

DAYDREAMERS

She might be one of the biggest pop stars on the planet, but Adele has a uniquely intimate relationship with her fans, who named themselves Daydreamers after her 2008 song "Daydreamer"—despite it being about unrequited love. Quite the contrary, the superstar and her fanbase share a mutual admiration. "I get pure shits and giggles from reading your tweets," she confessed during the Happy Hour with Adele Q&A session

live-streamed to Daydreamers around the world in 2022. More so, she appreciates the bond that superfans have created with each other. "It's really wholesome. I love it. It's just a joy to watch. Having 'stans' is quite a vibe."

The magnitude of "the lovely group" really hit Adele when she was forced to cancel her final two concerts at Wembley Stadium in 2017 after damaging her vocal cords. Hundreds of fans showed up anyway outside the venue to show their support as part of a grassroots gathering dubbed "Sing for Adele" that lit up social media. "It's fair to say that Adele could do with a pick-me-up right now," read a Facebook post for the event. "She's absolutely gutted. I think we should send her some love." They did just that, coming together to sing some of their favorite Adele songs, "Someone Like You" and "Hello."

When she returned to London in 2022 to perform for a hometown crowd of sixty-five thousand at Hyde Park, she recognized the superfans. At the end of the two-hour concert, Adele blew a kiss and said "Bye, Daydreamers."

EYELINER EVOLUTION

When teenage Adele stepped on the scene in 2008, her retro sound was punctuated with teased hair and cat-eye makeup. Ever since, winged eyeliner has been her signature, with some minor tweaks as she's evolved. The first time she tried the look was a year before the release of her album *19*—and it was completely unintentional. Adele had made an appointment with hair-and-makeup stylist Michael Ashton to trim her bangs, "and she asked if I could do a quick bit of eyeliner for her before she went to meet friends," he recounted to *Page Six* in 2021. "The eyeliner obviously got the

"I love her extreme talent. I love her writing. Her songs come from the soul."

seal of approval and the rest, as they say, is history . . . I don't think we ever would have thought it would become so iconic."

In the early years, Ashton put more emphasis on heavily lining Adele's upper and lower lids using a black pencil, with just a slight flick outward to create a cat-eye effect. Over time, he refined the look, thinning out the lining (especially on her lower lids) and concentrating more on the angled wing, which he creates in two steps: gel liner to get the shape and then a second layer with liquid liner (Adele's favorite is Pat McGrath Labs Perma Precision Liquid Eyeliner). "I think particularly the winged liner is just a look that suits her face so incredibly well because she has these big, beautiful almond-shaped eyes that she can really carry that off," Ashton told *CR Fashion Book*. "I think the other reason it's stood the test of time is that it's a very classic beauty look."

FAMOUS FANS

Some of the biggest names in Hollywood are proud Daydreamers: Adele's fanbase includes everyone from fellow hitmakers like Rihanna and Ed Sheeran to box office powerhouse Tom Cruise who was spotted at her 2022 concert in London's Hyde Park. "I don't think I've met someone who is *not* an Adele fan, to be honest," Selena Gomez mused to the Associated Press. "How can you not be? I think she's such an incredible, special artist." Celine Dion, one of Adele's childhood favorites, has gone as far as calling the "Easy on Me" singer one of the best of her generation. "I love literally everything about her," Dion told *Vegas* magazine. "I love her extreme talent. I love her writing. Her songs come from the soul." The queen herself has even covered a few at her own concerts, including "Rolling in the Deep" and "Hello."

Drake is also a certified fanboy. In 2018, when he found out Adele had attended his Los Angeles concert, he freaked out. "Thank god nobody told me. I would have been SHOOK," he wrote on Instagram. "I love this woman." The respect is mutual: Adele asked the rapper to preview *30* and give his honest opinion. "I'm like, 'Do you think this is like, what people want or not want?' And he was like, 'Absolutely,'" she said on the UK radio show Capital Breakfast. On the contrary, Adele cherishes her relationships with famous-fans-turned-friends from other industries, like actresses Cameron Diaz and Jennifer Lawrence. "They humanized me," she told *Rolling Stone*. "We never spoke about work, which was amazing, because most of the time when I catch up with someone, they want to know all about my work, and I'm like . . . Can we talk about something else? I'm knackered."

GLASTONBURY FESTIVAL

In the US, there's Coachella. In the UK, the most significant cultural event every year is Glastonbury, a five-day festival celebrating music and the performing arts located on 1,500 acres (607 ha) of farmland in Somerset, England. Like Coachella, Glastonbury draws crowds of 200,000-plus people to see the biggest names in pop and rock, like Beyoncé, The Rolling Stones, U2, Metallica, Coldplay—and Adele. In 2016, nine years after she first performed at the festival under a tent "to no one," the best-selling female artist of the twenty-first century returned to headline its legendary Pyramid Stage.

Adele kicked off her ninety-minute set with "Hello" and made her way through the biggest hits of her career, including "Rumour Has It," "Rolling in the Deep," "Set Fire to the Rain," and "Someone Like You." Just as entertaining was her stage banter, as she chatted with fans in the front row and even brought up a ten-year-old girl for a selfie. "Obviously I'm nervous and scared, hence why I'm talking a million miles an hour," she told the crowd (and another 18.7 million watching online). But by the end, she was in her element. "I didn't wanna come on and now I don't wanna go off. This is surreal. This is the best moment of my life."

On the fourth anniversary of her Glastonbury appearance, Adele slipped into the same custom-designed Chloe black silk, beaded dress to rewatch her performance on TV at home amid the COVID-19 lockdowns that canceled the 2020 festival, according to her Instagram.

HAIRSTYLES

Adele's hair is as big as her voice—but doesn't quite come along as naturally as her God-given talent. At the start of her career, the singer

A CLASS OF THEIR OWN

Adele's yearbook at the BRIT School reads like a who's who of the music industry. Among her 2006 graduating class at the performing arts high school in London were Grammy-nominated Jessie J and future *The X Factor* winner Leona Lewis. Adele was especially tight with the "Bang Bang" singer and the two would spend their lunch breaks serenading other students. "We just used to ad-lib and make stuff up," Jessie J recalled on the Australian radio show *Fitzy & Wippa with Kate Ritchie*. "Who knew [all this] would happen." Another famous BRIT alum is Amy Winehouse, who graduated several years before Adele. As recording artists, they ran in similar circles—but that was the extent of their friendship. The similarities between the two British blue-eyed soul singers followed Adele early in her career, and she always welcomed the comparisons. "I don't mind. I love Amy," she told *Hits* magazine in December 2011, five months after the "Back to Black" artist's tragic death from alcohol poisoning. "It means everything to me to be compared to Amy Winehouse."

often threw her hair up into a messy bun or low ponytail for an interview or performance when she was short on time. "Then we moved on to big hair" during the *21* beehive phase, her longtime stylist Michael Ashton told *Refinery29* in 2016. "We would use half wigs on tour because it shortened the amount of time we had to be in the hair and makeup chair—and then it stuck. Each had a name; one was called Jackie [after romance novelist Jackie Collins]. She really enjoyed big hair." Adele loved her wigs so much, she kept several at her home, although she had an unorthodox method of organizing them: in a 2012 interview with *60 Minutes*, Anderson Cooper was tickled to see her hairpiece collection strewn across a bed during a tour of her mansion in the English countryside.

Over the years, Adele's hair has changed along with her lifestyle. In 2015, the singer debuted what she called "a mum bob," a chin-length chic style that was easier to maintain while chasing after her son, Angelo. When she reemerged from hiatus in 2020 to host *Saturday Night Live* ahead of *30*, Adele's hair was the longest it had ever been, several inches past her shoulders. "This is all mine by the way," the wig-lover joked in her opening monologue, as she ran her hands over her blonde-highlighted hair, curled into an Old Hollywood style. She got even more experimental for her Weekends with Adele residency: ponytails, braids, curls, even a French twist.

INSTAGRAM LIVE

Adele's first (and, so far, only) time going live on Instagram was one for the pop culture books. In 2021, she hopped on the social media platform to chat with fans about her upcoming album, *30*, an event so "chaotic and iconic" (according to *Entertainment Tonight*), even CNN covered it as news. As questions came in fast and furious from many of her forty million followers, Adele struggled to keep up as they flashed across the screen. "I'm not very good at this stuff," she grumbled, as her long fingernails could be heard tapping away, eventually activating a filter that made animated algebra questions fly around her head.

There were plenty of gasps and moments of awkward silence as the "elder millennial" struggled to make sense of the technology. Then, there were the unfiltered questions: "What's my body count?" Adele read aloud, clearly unaware the fan was asking her number of sexual partners. "Is a hot dog a sandwich?" No. "Remember when a bat chased you in Mexico?" She did, and she recounted the story of how the winged mammal once swooped down on her during a concert. Several times over the forty-two-minute session, Adele's two dogs could be heard barking in the background. "Boys, boys," she yelled, "I'm on Instagram Live!"

JENNY

The singer went undercover as an Adele impersonator to fool a group of her biggest fans for an epic prank that aired on the BBC in 2015. Hosted by Graham Norton, the ruse is that he's auditioning tribute acts for his new show, *My Adele*—but what they also don't know is that the real Adele is among them, disguised as "Jenny" under a prosthetic nose and chin.

Backstage as they wait to be called up to sing, she makes small talk with the other impersonators, decked out in Adele-style black dresses and bouffant hairstyles. Naturally, the conversation turns to their favorite singer, as rumors swirl in the press that she's about to release the long-awaited *25*. "I can't wait for the new album," gushes one impersonator. "She's taken her time," quips Jenny, prompting chuckles from the unsuspecting group.

"I didn't wanna come on and now I don't wanna go off. This is surreal. This is the best moment of my life."

The last to audition is Jenny, who walks awkwardly to centerstage, fumbles with the mic stand, and misses her cue. But the jig is up the moment she finally starts to sing "To Make You Feel My Love." One by one, the impersonators suspect they recognize the famous voice. "That's Adele," someone gasps, as their jaws drop—and a few even break down in tears. The prank is just as popular nearly a decade later. On YouTube, the original video and a nine-minute extended clip have racked up more than a hundred million views.

KING CHARLES

The Brit has a complicated relationship with the royal family. In 2013, Adele was appointed as an MBE (Member of the Most Excellent Order of the British Empire) by Queen Elizabeth II for her contributions to music

"But it was just amazing, it was the best night ever."

and invited to Buckingham Palace to receive a medal from the future King of England, Prince Charles. In the televised ceremony, the beehived singer—dressed conservatively in a long-sleeved tea dress by Stella McCartney—curtsied as she approached the royal and laughed nervously as he pinned the medal on her lapel. "It was an honor to be recognized and a very proud moment to be awarded alongside such wonderful and inspirational people," Adele said in a statement afterward, referring to fellow recipients such as singer-songwriter PJ Harvey and *Chocolat* author Joanne Harris. "Very posh indeed."

A decade later, however, Adele changed her tune toward the scandal-plagued House of Windsor. When the Queen died in 2022, amid Prince Harry's estrangement from the royal family, Charles inherited the throne—and the new monarch wanted Adele to perform at his coronation celebration. According to reports, the singer turned down the request, as did Ed Sheeran and Harry Styles, but did not give an explanation. "[It] was a massive disappointment," an event organizer told *OK!* magazine. "They are titans of the showbiz industry and are quintessentially British but also known across the globe. It's such a shame."

LATER . . . WITH JOOLS HOLLAND

On June 8, 2007—six months before she released her first album—Adele made her TV debut on *Later . . . with Jools Holland*, a popular British musical television show she had watched since she was four years old. When another guest dropped out at the last minute, the completely unknown Adele was called in to perform, on the same episode as Beatles legend Paul McCartney, no less. "It was really, really frightening," recalled Adele, who sang "Daydreamer" while playing acoustic guitar. Even more nerve-racking, Adele followed Icelandic superstar Björk, one of her favorite singers.

Over the years, Adele has returned to Holland's program several times, including his 2008 New Year's Eve *Hootenanny* special and in 2011 to perform "Someone Like You." Looking back at her first appearance for the twentieth anniversary of *Later . . . with Jools Holland*, "I have the fondest memories of that, the whole [experience]," she said. "Meeting Jools, the hallways, the dressing rooms, the floor—it was so much bigger than . . . I always thought it was tiny, because everyone's always like 'studios are never as big as they look on TV,' but it was massive. But it was just amazing, it was the best night ever."

MR. 21

One man had the power to inspire the best-selling album of the twenty-first century, yet he has remained somewhat of a mystery. Adele has never publicly identified the ex who was the muse for "Someone Like You," "Rolling in the Deep," and the entire track list of *21*—but Internet sleuths have a pretty good idea, based on clues she dropped in interviews: Alex Sturrock. The photographer was hired to document her tour, An Evening with Adele, and his subject ended up becoming his secret girlfriend for about a year. Some of the behind-the-scene photos he snapped of the singer reveal her smoking in bed, holding a balloon that says "I Love You," and playing in the snow.

Sturrock is ten years older than Adele, just as she revealed, and his gritty art has been praised by *Vice* as "some of the best street photography we've seen in years." When talking about his impact on her, Adele told *Out* magazine in 2011: "We had everything—on every level we were totally right. We'd finish each other's sentences, and he could just pick up how I was feeling by the look in my eye, down to a T, and we loved the same things, and hated the same things, and we were brave when the other was brave and weak when the other one was weak . . . and I think that's rare when you find the full circle in one person, and I think that's what I'll always be looking for in other men." The following year, she was a little more clear-sighted when talking about her ex to *Vogue*. "He was great, but it was never going to work," she admitted to the magazine. "And the best thing is, I now know what I want for myself and from someone else. I didn't know what I wanted before."

NET WORTH

As one of the best-selling musical artists on the planet (120 million records and counting), Adele is also one of the wealthiest. The sixteen-time Grammy winner is worth a reported $220 million, based on royalties, tour revenue, merchandise, and various investments. It's estimated she earns an average of $60,000 a day from streaming alone—which adds up to approximately $22 million dollars annually. Adele's tours have always grossed big money ($278.4 million from Adele Live 2016), but she truly hit pay dirt with her Las Vegas residency, Weekends with Adele, the hottest ticket in town. During its two-year run, her residency reportedly grossed $2.2 million each night—and there were a hundred of them—for an estimated total of $220 million.

Over the decade between 2009 and 2019, Adele earned a reported $430 million. However, that same year she separated from Simon Konecki, and without a prenuptial agreement in place, the singer could have forked out over half her fortune per California law, the couple's primary residence. With their divorce settled in 2021, any income Adele generated from *30* and Weekends with Adele, were purely her own. In her relationship with Rich Paul, she remains the breadwinner, despite his own mega wealth as a sports agent: $120 million. Together, the power couple are worth nearly half a billion!

ONE NIGHT ONLY

Five days before the release of *30*, her first album in six years, Adele gave fans a sneak peek at a handful of the new tunes on her CBS primetime special, *One Night Only*, a private concert held at Griffith Observatory, a landmark atop Mount Hollywood. Indeed, the stars came out to witness

"It was definitely an out-of-this-world setting, that's for sure. I felt like a bloody movie star up there, I couldn't believe it."

Adele's first live performance in years, including Leonardo DiCaprio, Drake, Selena Gomez, Melissa McCarthy, Tyler Perry, Ellen DeGeneres, and CBS News broadcaster Gayle King—best friend of Oprah Winfrey—who also interviewed Adele for the special. Streamed simultaneously on Paramount+, *One Night Only* drew 10.33 million viewers, making it the most watched television event of the year. It was also nominated for five Primetime Emmy Awards, winning all categories including Outstanding Variety Special, Outstanding Directing, and Outstanding Lighting Design.

Adele had no idea how major the performance would be until the soundcheck. Driving up to the venue, set in the 4,300-acre (1,740 ha) Griffith Park, she was shocked by the closed roads and amount of security and park personnel. "What's all of this? This is gonna get in the way of

"In order for me to feel confident with one of my songs it has to really move me."

people coming to the show and stuff," she recalled on the *Audacy Check-In* podcast. When her driver explained it was for her concert, she was speechless. "It was such a big, bloody production. It looked beautiful. It was wild. It was definitely very overwhelming." But there was comfort in the intimate size of the crowd, which included her nine-year-old son, Angelo. "I think I would've probably thrown up had it been thousands of people. It was definitely an out-of-this-world setting, that's for sure. I felt like a bloody movie star up there, I couldn't believe it."

PETS

While men have come and gone, Adele has always had man's best friend in her life. In 2009, the singer adopted a dachshund she named Louis

Armstrong (Louie with an e, for short) after the influential jazz trumpeter. For nearly a decade, throughout the *19*, *21*, and *25* eras, the tiny pup was Adele's constant companion. He came along on world tours and was photographed with his famous owner for the pages of *Vogue* and *Nylon* magazines. Adele even released a Louie merchandise line of T-shirts, tote bags, and mugs featuring an illustration of the short-legged, long-bodied wiener dog. "Louie is the love of my life," she joked to the UK's *Daily Star* in 2011 while promoting *21*. "The third album will be all about him, I promise."

Instead, *25* was largely inspired by a different little guy in her life: her son, Angelo. On tour, Louie remained a loyal companion, always waiting backstage for the singer throughout Adele Live 2016. When she returned with *30* in 2021, however, Louie was noticeably absent—and Adele had two new dogs, goldendoodles (a crossbreed of golden retriever and poodle) named Freddie and Bob. "We call Freddie 'After-Party Freddie' because he always wants to do something when it's finished. And Bob loves a job," she told makeup artist Nikkie de Jager of the canine brothers. "They are such characters, it's hilarious. So yeah, my son and them keep me grounded."

Adele has yet to reveal the inspiration for their names, but fans speculate it could be another pair of legendary musicians: most likely Queen frontman Freddie Mercury and either Bob Dylan or Bob Marley.

QUEEN OF HEARTBREAK

With an entire catalogue of tearjerkers, it's no surprise that Adele has been crowned the "Queen of Heartbreak." During the songwriting process, she uses herself as an emotional guinea pig to test the power of lyrics. "In order for me to feel confident with one of my songs it has to really move me," she

explained to *The New York Times* during the *25* era. "That's how I know that I've written a good song for myself—it's when I start crying. It's when I just break out in [expletive] tears in the vocal booth or in the studio, and I'll need a moment to myself."

But it's Adele's ability to find the words that resonate with millions from all walks of life who have experienced a similar heartbreak that is truly impressive. "Her power or ability to turn something into a message that other people can understand is so important," producer Paul Epworth told *Billboard*. "She writes very close to the bone, and sometimes just says it in a way that hasn't been said before."

Each of her heartbreaks, from her first love on *19* to the end of her marriage on *30*, have brought their own distinct wave of emotions. And each time, Adele has grieved similarly, surrendering to the pain and then moving on. "I mope around for a little while," she confessed to *Entertainment Weekly*. "I do embrace the fact that I'm heartbroken. I don't move on quickly. I don't know if that's because it seems that I'm only really creative when I'm a bit momentarily depressed."

REAL ESTATE

Adele lived in a two-bedroom apartment located above a discount store in South London until she was eighteen. "It was the best house I've ever lived in," she told *British Vogue* in 2021, "[because] it was with my mum." In fact, Adele missed her mother so much after renting her own Notting Hill apartment that she moved back in with Penny Adkins for a brief period following the release of *21* in early 2011.

Later that year, the "Rolling in the Deep" singer sought tranquility at Lock House, a thirteen-bedroom estate nestled in the countryside of West Sussex that she rented for $17,200 per month. In 2012, she put down roots in the city and by the sea. Adele's very first piece of real estate was a $3.4 million oceanfront house with its own private stretch of beach just outside Brighton in the county of East Sussex. Fifty miles inland, she also purchased a pair of neighboring mews houses (row of carriage houses) worth $15 million in London's exclusive Kensington area, with the intention of combining the two into one mega-residence.

Across the pond, in America, the British singer set her sights on the West Coast. As she house-hunted, Adele rented a seven-bedroom Beverly Hills estate, once owned by Sir Paul McCartney, with its own bowling alley and wine cellar for an astounding $100,000 a month. In 2015, she snapped up her first piece of US property, a $5.2 million Mediterranean-style mansion in Malibu overlooking the Pacific Ocean. However, she didn't stay long, and in 2016, relocated her family back to the 90210 zip code—where she has remained ever since, accumulating an $80 million real-estate portfolio. The first property was a $9.5 million private retreat in the Hidden Hills gated community, with a two-story foyer, two formal living rooms (both with their own fireplaces), library, chef's kitchen, pool, and spa. Three years later, when Adele and husband Simon Konecki separated, she purchased a $10.65 million mid-century compound directly across the street from her ex, so they could easily co-parent son Angelo.

In 2021, she moved again, literally a stone's throw away, next door, into the former home of her friend Nicole Richie, who sold the 5,500-square-foot (511 m^2) renovated residence to the singer for $10 million in an off-market deal. The property's outdoor amenities are perhaps the biggest selling point: pool, jacuzzi, basketball court, dining patio, edible garden, and a chicken coop designed as a replica of the

"It was a huge moment in my life when they came out."

main house. But it would be a temporary space as she prepared her forever home.

In 2022, Adele and her now fiancé, Rich Paul, purchased a $58 million estate worthy of a Hollywood power couple: an Italian Riviera–style mansion formerly owned by Sylvester Stallone that boasts eight bedrooms, twelve bathrooms, a movie theater, a cigar room, a bar, a gym, a putting green, and sweeping city and canyon views, plus a life-size bronze statue of Stallone's iconic Rocky character that Adele insisted the actor leave behind or "that's gonna blow the whole deal," Stallone revealed to *The Wall Street Journal*. The singer and sports agent reportedly sunk several million into renovating the 18,587-square-foot (1,727 m^2) residence, ultimately demolishing it completely (but sparing a detached two-story guesthouse)

> *"I mean,
> I am a Lana fangirl,
> but not a crazy one."*

and rebuilding it to their specifications. The construction project is so extensive that, as of February 2025, Adele and Rich had yet to move into their love nest.

SPICE GIRLS

Adele's life was turned upside down when she first discovered the Spice Girls, the British quintet who brought "girl power" to the world in the late 1990s. "It was a huge moment in my life when they came out," she told James Corden in 2016. The two belted out the best-selling girl group's 1997 hit single, "Wannabe," as part of "Carpool Karaoke," a recurring segment on *The Late Late Show with James Corden*, in which he sings with musical guests as they drive around town. Adele also revealed that for her tenth birthday in 1998, she and four of her friends dressed up as their favorite

Spice Girl—Adele was "Ginger Spice," Geri Halliwell. Weeks later, the fiery redhead, best known for wearing a Union Jack dress, abruptly quit the group. "It was the first time I was truly heartbroken," Adele confessed to Corden.

Two decades later when the Spice Girls reunited (except for Victoria "Posh" Beckham), Adele not only got to see them perform at Wembley Stadium, but she also went backstage to meet the quartet: Ginger, Melanie "Scary" Brown, Melanie "Sporty" Chisholm, and Emma "Baby" Bunton. "I got drunk with the girls and quite frankly I can't believe how far I've come," Adele wrote on Instagram.

TATTOOS

Adele has more tattoos (twelve) than she does Top 10 hit singles (eight). Each holds special meaning, permanently inked on her body to commemorate her son, Angelo, mother, Penny, and even herself. She started off small, with three dots on the inside of her left wrist, which is believed to match one tattooed on Adele's good friend, singer Joy Williams (formerly of folk duo the Civil Wars). Below that, in 2011, she added a coin with the words "One Penny" in honor of her mother, although the tattoo is much larger than an actual one-cent penny.

The new mom celebrated the 2012 birth of her son, Angelo, with an "A" inked in cursive behind her right ear, which she debuted at the 2013 Grammy Awards. Months later, Adele reached out to celebrity tattoo artist Bang Bang—who has inked Rihanna, Justin Bieber, and LeBron James—to etch "Angelo" and "Paradise" on her right and left hands, respectively. As she later explained to *Rolling Stone*, "Angelo is my paradise." Coincidentally, Lana del Rey has a similar "Paradise" tattoo in

the same place. "She probably thinks I'm, like, some mad fangirl," Adele joked to the magazine. "I mean, I am a Lana fangirl, but not a crazy one." During her session with Bang Bang, she also inked a "5" on her finger. Her favorite number is also represented with five doves she has flying across her back.

In 2019, the thirty-one-year-old added a Saturn tattoo on her right arm that reflected her "Saturn return," which in astrology is when the planet returns to the degree it was the moment a person was born—and thus brings a monumental transformation that begins during their late twenties and can last two years. For Adele, that was during the making of *30*. "It's where I lost the plot," she told *Vogue*. "When that comes, it can rock your life. It shakes you up a bit: Who am I? What do I want to do? What makes me truly happy? All those things." That same year, she also got a tattoo of a small mountain range on the inside of her right wrist, as a reminder of what she's overcome and to keep working on herself. "Soon there will be another bloody mountain," she told CBC's Tom Power, "so I need to learn what the tools are to make my climb up the next mountain easier."

UK EXPAT

After nearly three decades in England, Adele emigrated to America in 2016. The decision was best for her family, she told *Vogue*, as her life in London was mostly confined to "a car or inside a building. I wanted fresh air and somewhere I could see the sky." Her quality of life as a mother to Angelo, then a toddler, was also a major factor. "In England, if you haven't got a plan with a young child and it's raining, you're fucked. And the kind of house I have in LA, I could never afford in London. Ever . . . I looked at houses. It's like hundreds of millions of pounds. I don't have that much money at all. I'd throw up," she told *Vogue*.

She does have a home in London, however, and spent a good amount of time there until COVID-19 in 2020. Once lockdown started, they remained in Los Angeles due to travel restrictions. Subsequently, Adele released *21* and then spent two years performing most weekends in Las Vegas, so their trips back home became less frequent.

While she has no immediate plans to return to the UK, there are some things that make her feel homesick. "I miss British humor," she said on *The Graham Norton Show*. "Our humor doesn't always travel, so I find myself having to explain my jokes. I miss the humor, I miss my family, I miss, you know, a lot of my condiments. I love a sauce! I love a sauce!" Luckily, she did find a store in Los Angeles where she can get some of her favorites, like salad cream, similar to mayonnaise, and Branston Pickle, a relish made from diced vegetables pickled in a sauce of vinegar, tomato, apple, and spices.

Adele hasn't lost her English accent either—nor has Angelo, despite spending most of his life in Los Angeles. "He goes to school with American kids and he sounds like me," she told Norton in 2022. She does occasionally correct her son's pronunciation of words, and he does the same with her, like when she once said "free" instead of "three." "He's a little bit more well-spoken than me."

VOCAL RANGE

She's the single greatest voice of her generation: Adele possesses a range spanning three octaves (some experts argue it's closer to four), from as low as B2 on "Million Years Ago" to as high as G#5 (G-sharp five) on

"I don't want to open my mouth and people be like, 'Oh, her voice is ruined.'"

"Hello." Technically, the only living female singers with a wider range are Mariah Carey and Celine Dion, two of Adele's idols. Classified as a mezzo-soprano—the second-highest female voice behind soprano—the Brit can belt, hold long notes, and jump octaves with ease. Technical prowess aside, she particularly stands out for her innate ability to emote, which elevates the drama of her sentimental ballads. Among the most difficult Adele songs to perform are "To Be Loved," "Hello," "Love in the Dark," "Turning Tables," and "Someone Like You."

In 2011, Adele suffered a vocal hemorrhage that could have ended her career. Her throat surgery to stop a benign polyp's bleeding was not only successful, but her pipes actually became stronger than ever—she *added* four notes to her upper register! "It does make your voice, like, brand-new," she told *Rolling Stone* of the procedure. "Which I actually

> *"There was an overwhelming epiphany that I had restored this beloved voice that would bring joy to and inspire millions of people."*

didn't like at first, because I used to have a bit of husk to my voice, and that wasn't there at first." After resting her voice for three months (during which she communicated by typing into a phone app), Adele made her comeback at the 2012 Grammys. The six-time nominee performed "Rolling in the Deep," and she was terrified of the public reaction. She told Apple Music's Zane Lowe that she recalled thinking, "I don't want to open my mouth and people be like, 'Oh, her voice is ruined.'" But when she sang the first few verses a cappella "and something came out, it was a pure relief."

Among those in the audience who got to witness the special moment was the man who had saved Adele's voice, Dr. Steven Zeitels. To hear his famous patient nail her comeback was something he would never forget, the renowned surgeon told the *Daily Mail*: "There was an overwhelming epiphany that I had restored this beloved voice that would bring joy to and inspire millions of people."

WEEKENDS WITH ADELE

In 2017, after touring for sixteen months across three continents, Adele was done. "Touring isn't something I'm good at," she confessed to fans in Auckland. "I don't know if I will ever tour again." Four years later, she found a way to perform live that best suits her needs: a Las Vegas residency, Weekends with Adele. Set to kick off in January 2022, tickets for the twenty-four shows went on sale the month before—and all one hundred thousand tickets sold out in a record-breaking six hours. However, the day before opening night at Caesars Palace, a tearful Adele announced in an Instagram video that she was postponing the residency due to production delays.

When the curtain finally rose in November 2022, she proved it was all worth the wait. "Thank you so much for coming back to me," Adele told the four thousand fans in attendance on opening night. "It looks just like I imagined it would." The two-hour set featured twenty songs from her four acclaimed albums, opening with "Hello" and closing with "Love Is a Game." In between, there was plenty of banter from chatty Adele, who wore a different black gown each weekend, custom-designed by the likes of Versace, Louis Vuitton, and Stella McCartney. Some audience members truly had her speechless, like Shania Twain, Lady Gaga—and her obstetrician. "Oh my God," Adele exclaimed mid-song as she ran over to hug him. "This is my doctor that gave birth to my baby!"

Due to high demand, Adele kept extending the residency's run, ultimately concluding in November 2024 after a hundred concerts.

According to reports, Weekends with Adele is among the highest-grossing residencies of all time and one of the most successful.

XL RECORDINGS

Just months after graduating from high school, Adele got her big break in 2006, when she signed with XL Recordings. But it almost didn't happen. When the British independent label reached out to the teenage singer to set up a meeting, she had never heard of them—so she simply ignored the email. "Oh, it's probably just an internet perv," Adele recalled thinking to the UK's *Daily Express*. A male friend convinced her XL was legit, but still came along with her for the meeting just in case—and the rest is history. "From the first time I met her, she had a unique kind of self-possession," XL owner Richard Russell told *The Guardian*, "like she knew where she was going with it."

XL was founded in 1989, a year after Adele's birth, originally to release rave and dance music. In 1997, the label found success with The Prodigy's third album, *The Fat of the Land*, which sold ten million copies thanks to No. 1 single "Firestarter." Over the following years, XL put out music from The White Stripes, Radiohead's Thom Yorke, and rapper M.I.A. until signing Adele (in partnership with Columbia Records for US distribution). After three best-selling albums, she left XL for Columbia in 2015 and signed a global deal with its parent company, Sony Music, which released 2021's *30*.

YOUTUBE

The visual evolution of Adele's career can be traced on her YouTube channel, which boasts 31.5 million subscribers. In addition to music videos for each of her hit singles, there are performances from her first US tour—when she was playing in smaller clubs like the 250-person Triple Door in Seattle—television appearances, behind-the-scenes studio footage, even a blooper reel from the rather somber "Easy on Me" video. In a backstage clip from the 2009 Grammys, where Adele took home Best New Artist, the baby-faced singer gushed about meeting Miley Cyrus, Snoop Dogg, and Justin Timberlake and revealed where she would put her new trophies (in the bathroom).

The most popular video is "Hello" with 3.1 billion views, followed closely by "Rolling in the Deep" with 2.5 billion views and "Someone Like You" with 2.2 billion views. "Hello" broke all kinds of records when it was released in October 2015, beginning with twenty-four-hour views: 27.7 million, surpassing Taylor Swift's "Bad Blood" (20.1 million). Within 87 days, it hit the billion mark, shattering the previous record of 158 days set by Psy's "Gangnam Style" in 2012. Elsewhere on YouTube, Adele set a new high for late-night shows in 2016 when her viral "Carpool Karaoke" appearance on *The Late Late Show with James Corden* became the most watched video with 67.6 million in just four weeks (eight years later, it quadrupled to 264 million).

ZODIAC SIGN

When Adele was born on May 5, 1988, the sun was positioned in Taurus. The singer's zodiac sign is synonymous with charm, ambition, dedication, stability, and resilience. Interestingly, it's also associated with the voice and throat, making Tauruses especially susceptible to colds, coughs, and laryngitis—the same ailments that plagued the singer before she had laryngeal surgery in 2011. Ruled by Venus, the planet of love, Tauruses

"I went on a couple dinners with people and I was like, 'oh hell to the no.'"

are in it for the long haul. As someone who seeks stability in all aspects of life, they long to find The One and settle down, not date around. Indeed, when Adele put herself back out there after her divorce, "I went on a couple dinners with people and I was like, 'oh hell to the no,'" she revealed to *On Air with Ryan Seacrest*. As fate would have it, soon after Adele met sports agent Rich Paul at a mutual friend's birthday party—and within a year of going public in July 2021, engagement rumors swirled (she officially confirmed the happy news in 2024).

According to Adele's birth chart, which is based on the precise moment she entered the world (8:19 a.m.), Cancer is her ascendant or rising sign—the sign that affects one's personality. Cancers are emotional, creative, nostalgic, and love nothing more than being at home, as do Tauruses, which would explain why Adele especially craves her private life in between albums—and prefers a concert residency over a world tour. As for her endlessly entertaining potty mouth, that could be attributed to the singer's moon sign (how someone expresses themselves), Sagittarius, a fire sign personified by humor, honesty, and bluntness.

Although Adele hasn't spoken about her zodiac sign, she seemingly embraces it: at a May 2024 concert in Las Vegas, a fan gave her a belated birthday gift, a mint green "Taurus" headband, which she happily wore for the rest of her performance of "When We Were Young."

BEST OF THE TWENTY-FIRST CENTURY

Billboard kicked off 2025 with its definitive best-of list of the twenty-first century (so far), and of course, Adele was a repeat performer. Named the best-selling female artist in the UK, the soulstress also ranked as the twelfth biggest artist on the planet, just behind fellow pop music divas Taylor Swift (No. 1), Rihanna (No. 3), and Beyoncé (No. 7). However, Adele beat out all the competition for Album With the Most Weeks at No. 1: *21*, which spent a record-setting twenty-four weeks on the *Billboard* 200 chart. Released in 2011, it also took No. 2 on the Best Albums of the Twenty-First Century, second only to Morgan Wallen's *Dangerous: The Double Album*. Adele's third album has its own claim to fame on *Billboard*'s "25 Chart Feats That Never Happened Until the Twenty-First Century." On December 12, 2015, *25* sold 3.38 million copies in its first week, which equates to 5.6 copies per second! Perhaps even more impressive, *25* sold more than twice the total of the Nos. 2 through 100 albums combined.

PART FOUR

Someone Like Her

A RELATABLE QUEEN

She may be one of the biggest superstars on the planet, but Adele is just like us! Perhaps it's her roots, born and raised in working-class South London—she's always been a down-to-earth, relatable queen who enjoys life's simple pleasures, like Beyoncé, McDonald's, and a few glasses of wine. Chatty yet blunt, she has a way of making the most distant stranger feel like a longtime friend, as many lucky fans can attest. During a 2016 appearance on "Carpool Karaoke" on *The Late Late Show with James Corden*, in between singing along to her own hits, Adele recounted a recent night out at a restaurant where the more she drank, the more generous she got with other diners.

"I'm not very in touch with the fame side of it. I don't chase none of that, and to be honest it doesn't interest me at all."

It all began when she was an hour early to meet her friend and "looking like such a loser," so she ordered a glass of wine, then a second. The liquid courage inspired Adele to walk over to a table of people who clearly recognized the Grammy winner. "Let me get your meal for you," she offered. Three more glasses of wine later, she apparently promised a different table of fans tickets to her sold-out Nashville concert—which she realized the next day when she found an email address in her coat pocket, while nursing a hangover. "That's what happens when I'm drunk," she quipped.

HAPPIER AT HOME

A wild night out is few and far between for Adele, a self-described "recluse" who has preferred an evening at home over the club long before she became a mom. At the 2011 MTV Video Music Awards, she was one of the most nominated artists, tying Katy Perry with three wins and capping off the night with a performance of "Someone Like You" for 12.4 million television viewers, the highest in VMA history. "But I felt pretty out of place and wished I was at home with my girlfriends," Adele revealed days later on *The Jonathan Ross Show*. "I'm not very in touch with the fame side of it. I don't chase none of that, and to be honest it doesn't interest me at all." Still, the general public remains fascinated by her, one of the most famous superstars on the planet, and that extra attention has made her appreciate private life at home all the more. There is one thing she misses: grocery shopping. "The joy of my life," she explained to makeup artist Nikkie de Jager in 2021. "Browsing those shelves, I just love it." But because she wants to avoid being photographed by the paparazzi, "the planning that goes into it is fucking exhausting. I'll do my Instacart [grocery delivery service] . . . and that's where my fun sort of ends."

She taught herself how to cook by reading *30-Minute Meals* by British celebrity chef Jamie Oliver, just like the millions of others who made the cookbook the fastest-selling nonfiction work of all time in 2010. Adele's best dish is an "incredible spicy pasta" that she insists "even Italians I know" have praised for its deliciousness she declared in an interview with *Vogue*. Her son Angelo's favorite is Sunday roast, a traditional meal consisting of meat, potatoes, and vegetables. However, hers is straight from the drive-thru of the world's most popular fast-food chain: McDonald's Big Mac, Chicken McNuggets, and fries. "That's my three-course," she told *British Vogue*. "I eat it at least once a week!"—and always with the most important, yet basic condiment. "I carry little [packets] of Heinz Ketchup everywhere with me, [a]bit like how Beyoncé

has hot sauce in her bag," she added, quoting the singer's famous lyric from 2016's "Formation."

DREAMS COME TRUE

Adele's love for Queen Bey is as fanatical as any other member of the Hive. She's been loud and proud about her absolute obsession since the first time she heard Destiny's Child at the age of eleven in 1999. A decade later, when Adele became a famous singer in her own right, she continued to gush about Beyoncé, now one of her music industry peers. "She's a huge part of my life," Adele confessed to *Q* magazine in 2011. "Everything I refer to has always got something to do with Destiny's Child or her. She just knows what she wants. She's in control of it all. She's classy. She's still totally fucking relevant. And just a nice person."

The year before, Adele finally got to meet her longtime favorite at a Grammys party—and she pretty much had the same reaction as anyone else. "I was like, 'Can I have a picture?' and Beyoncé said, 'Can I have a picture with you?'" she gushed, recalling the life-altering moment to *Q* magazine. Adele officially transitioned from fan to friend, and the two divas remained close over the years. In 2023, she dished on being invited to Jay-Z and Bey's exclusive Oscars after-party, an event so A-list that the sixteen-time Grammy winner was hardly the most famous attendee. But she did manage to stand out, as she recounted to fans at her Las Vegas residency days later. "It's so typical me trying to be glamorous in Hollywood. I got there, I give someone a hug [and] the sleeve rips off my dress." As she frantically tried to fix it, two of her nails broke. "I'm there with the coolest people in the world looking like an absolute tramp," she laughed.

It doesn't take much to bring the sentimental Adele to tears. As a kid, her "Grampy" promised to take her to Disneyland when she turned twelve, but he died of cancer before he got the chance. Sixteen years later, she got to realize a childhood dream when she visited the California theme park with her then three-year-old son—a full-circle moment that unlocked a core memory once she spotted Sleeping Beauty's iconic castle. "I was like full-on welled up," she confessed on *The Ellen DeGeneres Show*. "I was really emotional and just the whole thing, him believing—and me believing—that they were all real. The innocence of it all is what was so magical. I cried when I met [*Beauty and the Beast's*] Belle because I was talking to my kid and then she started talking and I was like, 'Oh my God!' She sounded just like the character from the film, and it freaked me out and I burst into tears."

ALL HER LOVE

The Queen of Heartbreak goes through the same highs and lows as the fans who identify with her deeply personal lyrics—and she's always worn her emotions on her sleeve. Adele was any other girl with a crush when CBS News first profiled the twenty-year-old singer in 2008. "She was constantly, sometimes frantically text messaging her new boyfriend—who wasn't texting back," *Sunday Morning* correspondent Anthony Mason reported in a voiceover, as Adele is seen rifling through her bag in search of her Blackberry. "Oh did you film that?" she exclaims to the camera, with a hearty cackle. "Me panicking, thinking I got a text."

A decade later, as she worked through the devastation of her 2019 split from her husband, Simon Konecki, the first step toward healing was "just knowing you're a hot mess," she admitted to Apple Music's Zane Lowe in

"She sounded just like the character from the film, and it freaked me out and I burst into tears."

2021. Fans especially appreciated Adele's candor, with one clip from the interview going viral on TikTok for being "one of the most relatable things she has ever said," according to the video caption. As Adele described it: "I could wake up and feel alright and feel like I was gonna have an alright day, and then like halfway through the day it would be like this massive rock would just fucking land on my head and squash me down, ya know?" She credited therapy with getting through the depressive episode, however, she admitted she stopped going after two years in order to figure some things out on her own. But she predicted to Lowe: "I'll probably need it again in three months."

Sure enough, when she announced her Las Vegas residency weeks later, it triggered a deep-seated anxiety with performing live. The day before opening night in January 2022, she postponed Weekends with

Adele. "I'm so sorry, but my show ain't ready," she tearfully told fans in an Instagram video. When the residency ultimately kicked off that November, Adele was up front about her mental health journey. "So I started having therapy again," she announced at her eighth performance, as supportive cheers filled The Colosseum at Caesars Palace. The last time, "obviously I was going through my divorce, and I was basically doing five therapy sessions a day," she said with a laugh. "But now I am doing it because I just want to make sure . . . I can give you everything."

    Adele fought back tears as she opened up about the mental progress she had made—and how fans were instrumental in her healing. "I love making music, but there is something about performing live that actually terrifies me and fills me with dread normally," she explained. "But this experience of being in a room this size, I think I might be a live artist for the rest of my life . . . Having the human interaction every weekend is honestly—I'm the happiest I've ever ever ever ever been."

THE SAME ADELE AT ANY SIZE

For many fans, the most relatable thing about the world-famous vocal powerhouse was that she represented the average woman (size 14 to 16), not the unrealistic body type projected by Hollywood. "I think I remind everyone of themselves," Adele reasoned to *Rolling Stone* in 2015. "Not saying everyone is my size, but it's relatable because I'm not perfect, and I think a lot of people are portrayed as perfect, unreachable, and untouchable." So when she revealed a one-hundred-pound (45 kg) weight loss in 2020, the public reaction was as dramatic as her transformation. Adele took the criticism in stride, explaining that her slimmed-down physical appearance was the unintended result of her mental metamorphosis. Following her split from husband Simon Konecki, she dealt with a "tsunami" of emotions—and hours spent at the gym improved her mindset. "I realized that when I was working out, I didn't have any anxiety. It was never about losing weight," she insisted to *Vogue*. "I understand why it's a shock . . . Visually I represented a lot of women. But I'm still the same person."

ADELE
UNFILTERED

One thing about Adele, she's going to say what's on her mind—and it's likely to include some colorful language. She's never been shy, either. In one of her first major interviews with *The Guardian*, the UK newspaper summed up the newbie: "At nineteen, Adele is a fully formed personality—exuberant, bawdy, disarmingly honest, effortlessly funny." *The New Zealand Herald* dubbed her "The Girl with the Mighty Mouth." On occasion, she has put her foot in it, which is why her management team eventually banned her from Twitter (now X) after a few too many drunk tweets (unfortunately, they've all been deleted).

"My life is full of drama, and I don't have time to worry about something as petty as what I look like."

Adele's account still exists, but if she wants to relay anything to her 27.1 million followers, someone else must post the message for her. "I don't have access to it, I don't know the passwords," she admitted to Swedish talk show host Fredrik Skavlan. "Because I might say something stupid."

Ahead of her performance at the Glastonbury Festival in 2016, Adele received a warning from the BBC about her potty mouth, which she later joked about to the crowd, saying, "the BBC had to give me a warning about my potty mouth." She responded by swearing thirty-three times throughout her ninety-minute set. The following year, at her Wembley Stadium show, Adele broke her own record with forty-four "f-bombs." "Fuck me, I've never been so fucking scared in all of my fucking life," she gushed to the sold-out crowd of ninety-eight thousand. "I don't know how to get my fucking nerves out. I'm shitting myself."

Adele credits her candor to a "gift of gab." As she explained onstage in 2023 at *The Hollywood Reporter's* Women in Entertainment gala, "I can absolutely talk for hours and eat your ear off, but when I talk for hours it's about nothing." Delivering speeches, on the other hand, "they're really not my fucking forte," she confessed as the crowd roared with laughter. "When I'm nervous I swear, forgive me." First and foremost, she thanked *The Hollywood Reporter* for bestowing her with the Leadership Award. "It's an absolute honor to be here . . . in full fucking glam at 8 a.m. on a Thursday morning. I'm just saying," she shrugged, "it's listed as a brunch; this is breakfast."

Adele is so unfiltered that she almost didn't recognize herself when she posed for a selfie with a filter-loving fan during a 2022 Las Vegas concert. "Oh my God, what have you done to my face?" the shocked singer exclaimed as she jumped out of the frame. "Why do you pick filters like that? We don't look like that, darling."

And she doesn't sound filtered, either. These are Adele's greatest unfiltered moments.

HOT AND UNBOTHERED

Adele's vocal range isn't the only thing that sets her apart from her peers in the music industry. Upon her debut in 2008, critics pointed out her weight, which she proudly proclaimed was plus-size. "My life is full of drama, and I don't have time to worry about something as petty as what I look like," she told *Rolling Stone* in 2011. "Even if I had a really good figure, I don't think I'd get my tits and ass out for no one. I love seeing Lady Gaga's boobs and bum. I love seeing Katy Perry's boobs and bum. Love it. But that's not what my music is about. I don't make music for eyes, I make music for ears."

NO. 2 PRIORITY

A collaboration between Adele and Beyoncé has the potential to broker world peace. Rumors swirled during the *25* era; however, the story was that Adele had turned down the opportunity to duet with her idol—and she was eager to set the record straight. "I would never disrespect her like that," Adele insisted to Apple Music's Zane Lowe. "Obviously, Queen Bey to the day I die." In an interview for the cover of *Time* in 2015, she doubled down: "Whoever started that rumor must be having a laugh because anyone who knows me knows that my main priority in life outside of my child is Beyoncé."

Four years later, Adele and Bey's shared music producer, Ryan Tedder, dropped a bomb when he told New York radio station Z100 that the divas had recorded vocals for a song on his band OneRepublic's forthcoming album *Human*, with Coldplay's Chris Martin on piano, no less. Turns out, it was just a cruel joke. Tedder clarified in an Instagram story that he had been "utilizing sarcasm"—yet fans did not see the humor.

GET OUT OF HER HAIR

As camera phones continue to improve, fans can snap Adele in increasingly high definition. But there's one thing she doesn't want them to capture when she's performing onstage in a dress: the hair on her legs. The singer decided to take a razor to them before a 2016 concert in Los Angeles because she worried those in the front row might notice she hadn't shaved for a month, she admitted in a *Vanity Fair* article. When the interviewer asked if her then-boyfriend Simon Konecki minded her hairy legs, Adele clapped back, "He has no choice. I'll have no man telling me to shave my fuckin' legs. Shave yours."

"...anyone who knows me knows that my main priority in life outside of my child is Beyoncé."

LOVER, NOT A HATER

Adele has made a career singing about heartbreak and its many stages of grief: denial ("Rumour Has It"), anger ("Rolling in the Deep"), bargaining ("Don't You Remember"), depression ("Hold On"), and acceptance ("Someone Like You"). Each album, she's always asked about the exes who inspired her lyrics, and depending on how much time had passed since the breakup, Adele would either be still bitter or able to look back with some sort of fondness. When "Mr. *21*" began sniffing around for royalties, she scoffed to the *Sun*, "He really thought he'd had some input into the creative process by being a prick. I'll give him this credit: he made me an adult and put me on the road that I'm traveling." By *25*, her "make-up album," she had found some inner peace. "For a while hate

"But I'm an adult now, I'm a mother, and I'm a lot less bitchy."

got in the way," she told *Vanity Fair* in 2016. "But I'm an adult now, I'm a mother, and I'm a lot less bitchy."

BATHROOM HUMOR

Adele was exceptionally chatty with the crowd of 150,000 at the Glastonbury Festival in 2016 and regularly checked on fans in the front row who had been standing there all day just to see her. But at one point during the show, the conversation turned TMI: "Have any of you had to go piss? Have any of you had to do a shit?" When one fan signaled to get the singer's attention, she walked over and asked, "Is there piss in that cup? You better not throw that at me." Turns out, bodily functions were on Adele's mind for a good reason. Ahead of her first Glastonbury performance, she received a warning from Coldplay's Chris

Martin: "Someone will try to throw something at you, probably a bottle of piss," Adele recalled to the BBC. "But it won't be spiteful. They'll just be off their face [drunk]."

MOTHER OF ALL CANDOR

To her son, Adele is simply mom, not the multiplatinum superstar she is to the rest of the world. That was never more apparent than when she took six-year-old Angelo to Taylor Swift's Reputation Tour in 2018. "His jaw dropped," she recalled to *Vogue*. "I got really annoyed! I was like, 'Excuse me! This is what I do, you know?' He said, 'When we go on tour, should I have a seat next to me with Taylor Swift's name on it for Taylor to come?'" In the same interview, Adele revealed that several older kids at Angelo's school had "chased him around" demanding to know if the rumors were true that his mother was Adele. "He was just like, 'I think her name's Adele, yeah . . .' He felt like he was being bullied because they were annoying him. I said, 'That's not bullying. Just say, 'Yeah, she's my mom. She wiped my ass!'"

A LEAGUE OF HER OWN

Good luck to anyone brave enough to attempt an Adele cover. "No one can sing my songs like me, period," she told *The Hollywood Reporter*—but her comment isn't exactly how it sounds. Adele explained that because she writes her own songs, she has a more genuine connection to the lyrics, which gives her an advantage. "I think I'm not the best singer in the world at all, but no one else can sing my songs like me because they didn't write them." However, after being reminded Aretha Franklin covered "Rolling in the Deep," she admitted the Queen of Soul was the exception to her rule.

"I'm just saying, they're never going to be able to emote it. Same way that I can't sing other people's songs. I didn't write the lyrics, and I can't sing [them] as well as them."

TO DRINK OR NOT TO DRINK

The "I Drink Wine" singer has been open about her dependency on alcohol and subsequent periods of sobriety, particularly during her 2019 divorce. "I was probably keeping the alcohol industry alive," Adele confessed to Oprah. In the summer of 2023, she decided to take a break from alcohol, which she revealed when she spotted a fan in the audience at Weekends with Adele drinking a whiskey sour. "It's boring. Oh my God, it's boring," she said about sobriety. "I mean, I was literally borderline alcoholic for quite a lot of my twenties. I miss it so much. Enjoy your whiskey sour, I'm very, very jealous." Sure enough, weeks later Adele announced she would be hopping off the wagon during a holiday break from her Las Vegas residency. "This is red wine weather," she told fans in November 2023. "I can't drink red wine ever when I'm singing because I don't know about you, but red wine fucks me up. I cannot handle it."

STFU OR GTFO

To Adele, the LGBTQ+ community has been "like my soulmates since I was really young." So when someone yelled out "Pride sucks!" at her residency in June 2024—the month of LGBTQ+ celebration—she did not mince words. "Did you come to my fucking show and just say that Pride sucks? Are you fucking stupid?" she admonished the offender, from the stage at Caesars Palace. "Don't be so fucking ridiculous. If you have nothing nice to say, shut up, alright?" Adele's allyship is much appreciated; however, it turns out she may have misunderstood the audience member. According to people sitting near the man in question, he called out "Work sucks!" in response to Adele bantering about how the weekend was the beginning of her work week. Either way, she made her point!

LEAST FAVORITE SONG

Adele's made up her mind: "Chasing Pavements" is her least favorite song. In August 2024, Adele performed her debut single for the first time in seven years, on opening night of her European residency, Adele in Munich. "The reason I don't sing this song very often, and I shan't sing it again after this Munich residency, is because the way I pronounced the words in this song when I was nineteen years old, I sound like I'm nineteen years old," the thirty-six-year-old explained to the crowd. "When I sing it now, I still sound nineteen years old and it annoys me. But I'm going to do it for you because I love you . . . the Germans have always been very, very loving to me."

SWEETEST DEVOTION

With little Angelo as her number-one priority, Adele has tailored her career in the best interest of her young son. She took off the first three years of his life, and when she returned with *25* in 2015, he came along for the ride, even on the road for her sixteen-month Adele Live 2016 world tour, which concluded just shy of his fifth birthday. There might not have been a third Adele album if it wasn't for Angelo, for whom she wrote "Sweetest Devotion." At the height of *21*, which she has described as "pandemonium," the fame-averse superstar felt overwhelmed by her own success and considered walking away completely. But when she became a mother, "it made everything all right, and I trusted everything because the world had given me this miracle," she told *Rolling Stone* in 2015. "All the things I really like about myself, he brings out in me, and he's the only person that tells me no. He completely rules me. He's the boss of me, and it's so funny for other people to watch, because I'm the boss of everything in my work life."

ANATOMY
OF AN ARTIST

Adele's natural-born talent was honed by studying the unique skill sets of her favorite singers. From jazz-blues icons Etta James and Ella Fitzgerald to gifted lyricist Lauryn Hill and the acrobatic Pink, young Adele picked up specific traits from each that she applied to her own artistry. The result was a blend of old school and contemporary—a timeless sound that has continued to evolve over each of her four albums. And she won't ever change to fit a mold. During the making of *30*, several times her team brought up concern that the album wouldn't resonate with teenagers on TikTok. "If everyone's making music for the TikTok, who's making the music for my generation?" she demanded in a November 2021 interview with Zane Lowe for Apple Music. "I will do that job gladly."

VOICE

Adele started singing as a little girl, mostly to entertain her mother's friends. But it wasn't until her teens that she actually found her voice—and at the bottom of a bargain bin, no less. Adele was browsing jazz CDs at her local music store in London when she was drawn to the vintage 1960s styling of two female icons, Etta James and Ella Fitzgerald. When she got home and pressed play, "my whole perception of what a voice could be completely changed," she told *The Daily Telegraph*. Until then, Adele had only taken one singing lesson, and it "made me think about my voice too much. You can teach yourself." And she did just that: Every night before bedtime, she spent an hour studying some of the greatest vocal talents in music history. "I listened to Etta to get a bit of soul. Ella for my chromatic scales." To learn how to control her powerful pipes, she researched "Killing Me Softly with His Song" singer Roberta Flack. Inadvertently, Adele's idols also influenced her English accent. "It depends on the kind of artists you love. My favorites are American artists," she explained to *Hits* magazine in 2011. "So there are obviously major traces of them in my voice."

SONGWRITING

A decade before she became the Queen of Heartbreak, Adele got a valuable lesson on the topic in 1998 when her mother came home with brand-new music: Lauryn Hill's *The Miseducation of Lauryn Hill*, a concept album about

> *"You have to write about real life because otherwise how can you be relatable?"*

the education of love. Adele distinctly remembers borrowing it from her mother and "analyzing" the lyrics for a solid month. "I was constantly wondering when I would be that passionate about something, to write a record about it—even though I didn't know I was going to make a record when I was older," she recalled in a 2011 interview with the now-defunct streaming service Rhapsody.

In celebration of *The Miseducation of Lauryn Hill's* twentieth anniversary in 2018, Adele thanked Hill for "the wisdom" in an Instagram ode describing the Grammy-winning album as "such an honest representation of love and life, I feel I can relate too." As a songwriter, she also strives to strike an emotional chord with her audience. "You have to write about real life because otherwise how can you be relatable?" Adele revealed to *The New York Times*.

"I remember sort of feeling like I was in a wind tunnel, her voice just hitting me. It was incredible."

STAGE PRESENCE

Adele has always had anxiety about performing live, but sometimes all she needs to do is summon some "girl power." The Spice Girls, one of her greatest inspirations, particularly influenced "the performance side of it, which I'm not actually that great at," she said in a 2008 interview with the BBC. "I can't move around stage very well, I feel a bit uncomfortable."

Another high-energy artist who exemplified how to command an audience and control her powerful voice is Pink. One of Adele's earliest defining moments was when she was fourteen and saw the "Get the Party

Started" singer in a concert at London's Brixton Academy in support of her debut album, *Missundaztood*. "I had never heard, being in the room, someone sing like that live," she recalled to *Spinner* in 2010. "I remember sort of feeling like I was in a wind tunnel, her voice just hitting me. It was incredible."

As an artist, she took a cue from Radiohead on what *not* to do. Adele went to see the British rock band in concert and was "so annoyed" when they didn't play their biggest hit, "Creep." (Radiohead singer Thom Yorke has admitted they're "tired of it.") "I get it, I get it," she said at the 2022 Happy Hour with Adele fan event, "but I would never do that, just because of how pissed off I was." On second thought, she joked, "ask me again when I'm sixty."

COMEBACK

In 2014, two years into Adele's hiatus, she went to see Kate Bush's London residency, her first series of shows in three decades—and the experience inspired her own comeback, *25*. The "Running Up That Hill" singer had stepped away from music (and the public eye) following her 1993 album, *The Red Shoes*, and then retreated even further after the birth of her son in 1998. It would be another seven years before Bush returned with the double album *Aerial*. Adele, who became a mother herself in 2012, didn't want to follow the same path. "I read somewhere, and I don't know if it's true or not, that [her son] said when he was sixteen, 'I want to know now why everyone loves you.' And it makes me so emotional," she confessed to *The New York Times*. "After that show, it was: 'I don't want to wait. I don't want to wait till my kid is sixteen, I want to show him now.'"

MEME MATERIAL

Adele was born with insane vocal talent . . . and an expressive face that could launch a thousand memes. Her authentic reactions to the most basic things—an unfunny joke, hearing a favorite song, being confused by technology, yawning at an inopportune moment—have all gone viral for their unintentional hilarity. "It's hard work being a constant meme," she joked during a Weekends with Adele concert in 2023. "I don't know what it is about myself . . . Maybe it's because I haven't had any Botox or anything. My face just moves so much."

She's given us so much material over the years, it seems there's a photo or GIF for every occasion, even divorce. When the singer returned to Instagram in 2019, following the news of her split from husband, Simon Konecki, she broke the ice (and the Internet) with an Adele meme: side-by-side photos of herself, one crying and the other looking confident, with the caption, "When you catch yourself in your feelings then you remember who you are."

WHEN YOU'RE JUST LOOKING FOR MICHAEL JORDAN

Since dating NBA super agent Rich Paul, the Brit has frequently popped up at one of the last places we ever expected her: courtside at basketball games. Her most memorable attendance was at the 2022 NBA All-Star event in Cleveland, where TV cameras fixated on "Adele, musical artist," as identified by the onscreen chyron. But instead of waving to viewers at home or showing her team spirit, Adele avoided all eye contact, looking aimlessly around the arena with pursed lips for fourteen awkward seconds. The clip was a slam dunk on Twitter (now X), where users added their own LOL-worthy captions, such as "me pretending not to see my grandma opening her wallet to give me money" and "me watching all the tables who ordered after me get they food first."

On the two-year anniversary, Adele broke her literal silence about "that viral meme of me looking like I don't give a flying fuck" during a concert in Las Vegas. She explained to the audience that she was sitting by herself while her boyfriend talked to athletes on the court. "And I was fine. I was just there on my own looking for Michael Jordan." That's when a camera crew approached and asked if they could film her—which she politely declined not once, but twice. Still, they did it anyway. As for her

> *"And I was fine.*
> *I was just there on my own*
> *looking for Michael Jordan."*

pained expression as she looked everywhere but at the camera, "I was sulking because I was like 'these motherfuckers . . .' and I didn't realize they were airing it on TV. I thought it was just [the Jumbotron]."

WHEN YOU KNOW EVERY WORD TO NICKI MINAJ'S "MONSTER"

It's one thing to go viral on the Internet, but it's another to do it on late-night television. In January 2016, Adele made her first appearance on "Carpool Karaoke," on *The Late Late Show with James Corden*. During their ride around London, the longtime pals chatted about her new album, *25*, and sang along to several tracks, as well as some of her favorites by other artists—most memorably Nicki Minaj's rap in Kanye West's "Monster." Adele delivered every rapid-fire lyric to perfection, complete with hand

gestures and plenty of attitude that made Minaj proud ("#Iconic," tweeted the rapper).

Within five days, Adele's "Carpool Karaoke" racked up 42 million views on YouTube, making it the most popular video on late-night since *Jimmy Kimmel Live* premiered the *Captain America* trailer in 2013 (31 million views in the first week). By the end of 2016, its numbers had more than tripled to 135 million to become the year's most viral video, beating out Channing Tatum's *Lip Sync Battle* performance of Beyoncé's "Run the World (Girls)" by 100 million. Adele's karaoke clip, bolstered by "Monster," has only proved its pop culture relevance: As of 2025, it has 266 million views. In 2023, she returned to "Carpool Karaoke" on *The Late Late Show with James Corden* for one last ride before Corden's show went off the air. More somber in tone, the two tearfully reflected on their friendship in between renditions of Adele's greatest hits, "Rolling in the Deep," "Hometown Glory," and "I Drink Wine."

WHEN YOU REFUSE TO COLLABORATE WITH PEPPA PIG

Adele on Instagram Live is real-time hilarity! In 2021, during a Q&A with fans about her new album, a one-word answer to a not-so-burning question ignited a firestorm with an animated piglet beloved by preschoolers in two hundred countries. "Am I gonna collab with Peppa Pig?" Adele read off the screen. "No!" Quick-thinking fans clipped the four-second moment and blasted it out on Twitter (now X), where it was liked and retweeted by tens of thousands, many of whom sided with Peppa. "@Adele just dropped some devastating news about her new album," wrote one person. "We really lost," lamented another.

"Any time you wanna go jumping in muddy puddles, I'm with ya, babes."

Days later, during the singer's virtual appearance on London's Capital FM, none other than Peppa herself called in to confront Adele about the apparent diss. "That made me really, really sad when you said you wouldn't collaborate with me," confessed the animated pig between snorts. "Why not? Don't you like me?" Adele couldn't believe her ears, as she looked around in shock. "Peppa, I've already said today, I regret it. I spent three years watching you," she added, in reference to her young son, Angelo. "I really, really regret it, and any time you wanna go jumping in muddy puddles, I'm with ya, babes. I felt terrible the second I said it."

Adele isn't the first celebrity to have beef with Peppa. In 2019, Iggy Azalea tweeted her annoyance that the popular pig's debut album was dropping the same day as her second, *In My Defense*. "Peppa's so fancy, you already know," mocked the cartoon's official Twitter (now X) account.

"Collab with me now," replied the rapper, "or you'll end up a breakfast special Peppa." They didn't, and Iggy's concern proved legitimate: Peppa's *My First Album* reached No. 6 on the UK Independent Albums chart, while *In My Defense* peaked at No. 35. The following year, Peppa was on the receiving end of another female rapper's rant when Cardi B complained her two-year-old daughter had ruined her Ugg boots by jumping in puddles just like the animated character. "Count your fuckin [sic] days," Cardi joked on Twitter (now X).

WHEN YOU GO TO THE SUPER BOWL JUST FOR RIHANNA

Adele was spotted at the 2023 NFL Super Bowl, but she wasn't there to root for the Kansas City Chiefs or Philadelphia Eagles. "I'm going just for Rihanna," she told a fan at a Weekends with Adele show. "I don't give a flying fuck who's playing." Indeed, any time the camera cut to her in the crowd, the British singer looked quite bored. Twitter (now X) pounced on the LOL moment, generating memes of the "unbothered queen" sipping a cocktail and wearing sunglasses. One tweet that received more than twenty-five thousand likes joked about Adele's possible confusion about American and English football: "I fought dis gayme was plaid wit ya feit" (read in Adele's accent).

She perked up at halftime as Rihanna prepared to take the stage. In another video clip that made the rounds on social media, Adele seemingly shushed those around her in anticipation of Ri's performance, but without audio it was anyone's guess what she was saying. "We need that lip translator from TikTok on this stat," quipped one tweet that was viewed more than fifty-two thousand times. The following weekend at her Las Vegas residency, the performer answered the Internet's burning

question—and it was quintessential Adele. "I was saying [Rihanna's] gonna be fine. She's gonna like have some weed and be fine. But clearly she couldn't have any weed because she's pregnant!"

The following year, the Super Bowl was played at Allegiant Stadium in nearby Paradise, Nevada, but Adele had no plans to attend a second time. "I realized when I was there, it's not really put on for the people in the stadium," she told the Weekends with Adele audience. "I couldn't see [Rihanna]. Maybe I had bad tickets, I don't know." She had better seats for Usher's 2024 halftime performance: "I'm going to watch it on TV."

WHEN YOU THINK NO ONE CAN SEE YOU BEHIND A TINY PURSE

Adele has said many times she doesn't like listening to her own music and has even gone as far as asking drivers to turn the channel the moment she recognizes a song. So imagine her cringe when she had nineteen thousand pairs of eyes on her as "Easy on Me" played throughout the Staples Center during an October 2021 Los Angeles Lakers game. The mortified superstar instinctively covered her face with a Louis Vuitton purse as TV cameras zoomed in on her sitting beside her fiancé, Rich Paul.

Adele's three minutes and forty-five seconds of embarrassment delighted social media, as photos of her pained expression behind the purse spawned reaction memes, like "rent trying to make eye contact with me." All these years later, photos of Adele hiding behind her Louis Vuitton are still relevant any time someone wants to admit to their own personal cringe, which for one gamer translated to: "Not me spending hours playing Roblox."

ADELE'S PLAYLIST

The pop-soul singer's musical tastes are as diverse as her own catalog. Many of Adele's early inspirations, like Etta James and the Spice Girls, remain in heavy rotation. Over the years, she's also discovered several new artists who wowed her with their voices (Brittany Howard of Alabama Shakes), lyrics (Lana del Rey), and ability to make her cry (Mumford & Sons). These are some of Adele's favorite songs to add to your own playlist!

"SALVATORE" — LANA DEL REY

Lana is a melancholy girl after Adele's own heart! "I'm obsessed with her. Her lyrics are fierce," Adele gushed to *Vogue*. But there's something about "Salvatore" on 2015's *Honeymoon*, which Adele blasted during her photoshoot with the magazine. "The chorus of this song makes me feel like I'm flying, like that bit in your life when it goes into slo-mo. When you've got nothing to do and you're staring out of the window and your mind goes to magical places."

"NEVER TEAR US APART" — INXS

The Australian rock band's 1988 ballad is "my favorite song ever," Adele told *Variety* in 2011, when she recorded a cover for *21*. As it turned out, her connection to the track didn't translate in the studio. "I was devastated because I sounded so unconvincing in it. I didn't believe a word I was singing." Still, she could never tear herself apart from the love song, iconic for its saxophone solo. "I still play it to myself," Adele said, and there were even rumors she re-recorded it for *25*.

"SPICE UP YOUR LIFE" — SPICE GIRLS

Adele's obsession with the iconic girl group is no secret, and their 1997 anthem for world unity is a timeless musical message. On tour in Amsterdam in 2016, the British singer teased fans with a few a cappella bars of the chorus. Three years later, she lived a childhood dream when she saw the reunited Spice Girls at Wembley Stadium. Backstage with friends, she led a rousing rendition of "Spice Up Your Life," a moment she documented on Instagram.

"I was devastated because I sounded so unconvincing in it. I didn't believe a word I was singing."

"I CAN'T MAKE YOU LOVE ME" — BONNIE RAITT

Adele loves the 1991 heartbreak ballad so much, she wishes she'd written it herself. "I Can't Make You Love Me" got her through the breakup that inspired *21*, and she's covered it several times, including at the Royal Albert Hall in 2011. "It makes me really, really happy and really, really devastated and depressed at the same time," she told the audience. "It makes me think of my fondest and best times in my life, and it makes me think of the worst as well . . . but I do love this song."

"AFTER THE STORM" — MUMFORD & SONS

Adele arrived on the scene at the same time as the London rock band Mumford & Sons. Their debut album, 2009's *Sigh No More*, is a bittersweet memory of her relationship with "Mr. *21*." "We blossomed to that record, and we died to that record," she told *Entertainment Weekly*. The closing track, "After the Storm," is so beautiful "it kind of makes me cry and smile at the same time." Adele would love to collaborate with lead singer Marcus Mumford, she told the *Sun*, because "his voice goes straight through me."

"ALL I COULD DO WAS CRY" — ETTA JAMES

The legendary singer is one of Adele's earliest influences, and she's remained her go-to over the decades. Any time she's dealt with heartbreak, "All I Could Do Was Cry" has been on heavy rotation. The 1960 doo-wop tune was inspired by real-life emotional pain: it was cowritten by Gwen Gordy, who married James's ex-boyfriend that same year. "Everything she sings, you believe her, even if she never wrote a word of it herself," Adele told *The Guardian* in 2011, the year before James died from leukemia.

"DON'T WANNA FIGHT" — ALABAMA SHAKES

Everything about the blues-rock band's singer Brittany Howard inspires Adele, and when she first heard "Don't Wanna Fight" off their 2015 album, *Sound & Color*, "I almost had to pull over . . . blew my mind," she marveled to *The Guardian*. "Brittany comes in with a scream. I'd love to experiment more with my own voice like that." Alabama Shakes went their separate ways in 2018, but Howard has enjoyed a successful solo career—and Adele's admiration. "There's something about Brittany that puts fire in my soul."

"SO FAR AWAY" — CAROLE KING

Songwriters recognize songwriters: King's *Tapestry*—which was inducted into the Grammy Hall of Fame in 1998—is "my favorite album ever," Adele told Oprah's *O, The Oprah Magazine*, with "So Far Away" as a standout track. "The emotions in her songs are beautiful." King wrote "So Far Away" in 1970 while on tour and missing her husband, and it's been covered by Pink and Rod Stewart. Adele, however, tried her hand at a different *Tapestry* classic, "(You Make Me Feel Like) A Natural Woman," on *VH1 Unplugged* in 2011.

"LITTLE BIT OF RAIN" — KAREN DALTON

Adele discovered the late country-blues singer Karen Dalton when she covered Bob Dylan's "To Make You Feel My Love." As she searched more into his backstory, she found Dalton, who played with Dylan during his rise in the 1960s Greenwich Village folk music scene. "There's not a lot of her music out there, she died quite young," Adele told *The Guardian* of Dalton, who released two albums before her tragic passing at fifty-five. "But her voice! Something haunting there, even eerie . . . Listen to ['Little Bit of Rain'] and you'll understand."

"DREAMS" — GABRIELLE

The very first song she remembers hearing as a child, "Dreams," is an inspirational pop-R&B tune that went straight to No. 1 on the UK charts in 1993, when Adele was five. "I think the lyric 'dreams can come true' is so infectious," she said on BBC Radio 4's *Desert Island Discs*. Adele got to meet Gabrielle in 2022 when she opened for her in London—and she was so starstruck by her childhood favorite, she cried. "She just made my day," Gabrielle told the *Daily Mail*. "She's incredible."

ACKNOWLEDGMENTS

She might be the Queen of Heartbreak, but Adele made me fall in love with her all over again while writing this book. Looking back at her earliest interviews (thank you, Internet Archive), she was just as unfiltered at *19* as she was at *30*, whether she was chatting about ex-boyfriends and drinking too much or expressing her lifelong passion for the Spice Girls. Adele's music has matured over the years, yet she remains the same international treasure.

ABOUT THE AUTHOR

Kathleen Perricone is a biographer with published titles about Marilyn Monroe, John F. Kennedy, Anne Frank, Barack Obama, Taylor Swift, Harry Styles, Beyoncé, Lady Gaga, Zendaya, Billie Eilish, Timothée Chalamet, and dozens more. Over the past two decades, Kathleen has also worked as a celebrity news editor in New York City as well as for Yahoo!, Ryan Seacrest Productions, and for a reality TV family who shall remain nameless. She lives in Los Angeles.

© 2025 by Quarto Publishing Group USA Inc.
Text © 2025 by Kathleen Perricone

First published in 2025 by Epic Ink, an imprint of The Quarto Group,
142 West 36th Street, 4th Floor, New York, NY 10018, USA
(212) 779-4972 • www.Quarto.com

All rights reserved. No part of this book may be reproduced in any form without written permission of the copyright owners. All images included in this book are original works created by the artist credited on the copyright page, not generated by artificial intelligence, and have been reproduced with the knowledge and prior consent of the artist. The producer, publisher, and printer accept no responsibility for any infringement of copyright or otherwise arising from the contents of this publication. Every effort has been made to ensure that credits accurately comply with information supplied. We apologize for any inaccuracies that may have occurred and will resolve inaccurate or missing information in a subsequent reprinting of the book.

Epic Ink titles are also available at discount for retail, wholesale, promotional, and bulk purchase. For details, contact the Special Sales Manager by email at specialsales@quarto.com or by mail at The Quarto Group, Attn: Special Sales Manager, 100 Cummings Center Suite 265D, Beverly, MA 01915 USA.

10 9 8 7 6 5 4 3 2 1

ISBN: 978-0-7603-9688-9

Digital edition published in 2025
eISBN: 978-0-7603-9689-6

Library of Congress Control Number: 2024953052

Group Publisher: Rage Kindelsperger
Senior Acquiring Editor: Nicole James
Creative Director: Laura Drew
Managing Editor: Cara Donaldson
Editor: Keyla Pizarro-Hernández
Cover and Interior Design: Beth Middleworth
Book Layout: Danielle Smith-Boldt
Illustrations: Lauren Mortimer

Printed in China

This publication has not been prepared, approved, or licensed by the author, producer, or owner of any motion picture, television program, book, game, blog, or other work referred to herein. This is not an official or licensed publication. We recognize further that some words, models' names, and designations mentioned herein are the property of the trademark holder. We use them for identification purposes only.